Contents

Unit		Unit	
	Introduction	35	Multipl... ...sion
1	Counting in Small Steps	36	Remainders and Rounding
2	Odds and Evens	37	Problems 7
3	Multiples	38	Multiplying by 2, 5 and 10
4	Problems 1	39	Multiplying by 3, 4, 6 and 8
5	Place Value	40	Dividing by 2, 5 and 10
6	Number Sequences	41	Dividing by 3 and 4
7	Number Ordering	42	Double Quick
8	Calculating with Multiples of 10	43	Quick Halves
9	Rounding to 10 and 100	44	Problems 8
10	Rounding to 1000	45	Multiplying by 10 and 100
11	Problems 2	46	Doubling and Halving Short Cuts
12	Fractions	47	More Multiplication Short Cuts
13	Comparing Fractions	48	Using Multiplication Short Cuts
14	Finding Fractions	49	Problems 9
15	Problems 3	50	Tally Charts and Frequency Tables
16	Addition and Subtraction	51	Bar Charts
17	Addition and Subtraction Facts	52	Venn Diagrams
18	Addition and Subtraction to 100	53	Carroll Diagrams
19	Facts to 50, 60, 70, 80, 90	54	Problems 10
20	Problems 4	55	Length, Mass and Capacity
21	Small Differences	56	Measuring with Decimals
22	Five and a Bit	57	Scales
23	Adding Tens and Units	58	Problems 11
24	Cheating with 10	59	Units of Time
25	Near Doubles	60	Reading the Time
26	Adding Several Numbers	61	Calendars
27	Number Patterns	62	Problems 12
28	Using Place Value 1	63	2-D Shapes
29	Using Place Value 2	64	3-D Shapes
30	Problems 5	65	Symmetry and Reflections
31	Adding with Pencil and Paper 1	66	Position and Movement
32	Adding with Pencil and Paper 2	67	Coordinate Grids
33	Subtracting with Pencil and Paper	68	Right Angles and Half Right Angles
34	Problems 6	69	Problems 13

Introduction

Each page of Maths Express has work on one topic.

First there is a quick introduction to the topic that shows how to do the exercises. There is sometimes a drawing to help you.

Last of all there is a Challenge section. This should be quite difficult and might take longer than the rest of the page. You might need help with some of it.

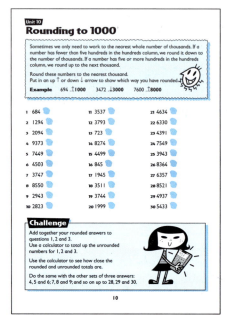

Then there are about 30 questions – your teacher may not want you to do all of them.

The Problem pages have word problems on them.
Read very carefully!

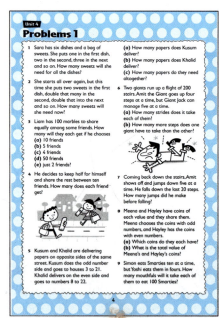

You should do your work in your own book. Remember to copy the questions carefully.

Unit 1
Counting in Small Steps

Count forward or backward for 4 more numbers.

Example   forward in 3s from 9   9, 12, 15, 18, 21

Rulers marked in centimetres (cm) make excellent number lines.

0 1 2 3 4 5 6 7 8 9 10 11 12 13 14 15 16 17 18 19 20 21 22 23 24 25 26 27 28 29 30

1 forward in 2s from 32
2 back in 2s from 18
3 forward in 4s from 40
4 back in 3s from 18
5 forward in 3s from 27
6 back in 4s from 36
7 back in 2s from 39
8 forward in 2s from 37
9 back in 3s from 66
10 forward in 4s from 148
11 back in 4s from 38
12 forward in 2s from 342
13 back in 3s from 127
14 forward in 3s from 236
15 back in 2s from 180
16 forward in 4s from 655
17 back in 4s from 232
18 forward in 3s from 267
19 back in 3s from 83
20 back in 2s from 179
21 forward in 4s from 765
22 back in 3s from 711
23 forward in 4s from 487
24 back in 3s from 944
25 back in 2s from 507
26 forward in 3s from 389
27 forward in 2s from 597
28 forward in 2s from 893
29 back in 3s from 882
30 forward in 4s from 613

Challenge

Start at 0 and keep adding 3 until you get to 60.
Look at the units in each number.
Can you see a sequence?
Do all the numerals 0 to 9 appear in the units?

Do the same again, but starting at 2 until you reach 62.
Do the units have a sequence this time?

Experiment with adding on 2s and 4s.
Do you get different sequences?
Does each sequence use all the numerals from 0 to 9?

Unit 2
Odds and Evens

Complete these sequences of numbers. At the end of each sequence, put a letter **O** for **odd** or a letter **E** for **even**. Be careful – some go backwards, some forwards.

Example 6, 8, 10, **12, 14, 16, 18** E   21, 23, 25, **27, 29, 31, 33** O

1. 5, 7, 9, ▢, ▢, ▢, ▢
2. 13, 15, 17, ▢, ▢, ▢, ▢
3. 8, 10, 12, ▢, ▢, ▢, ▢
4. 27, 29, 31, ▢, ▢, ▢, ▢
5. 32, 34, 36, ▢, ▢, ▢, ▢
6. 46, 48, 50, ▢, ▢, ▢, ▢
7. 55, 57, 59, ▢, ▢, ▢, ▢
8. 38, 40, 42, ▢, ▢, ▢, ▢
9. 77, 79, 81, ▢, ▢, ▢, ▢
10. 18, 16, 14, ▢, ▢, ▢, ▢
11. 19, 17, 15, ▢, ▢, ▢, ▢
12. 28, 26, 24, ▢, ▢, ▢, ▢
13. 66, 68, 70, ▢, ▢, ▢, ▢
14. 79, 77, 75, ▢, ▢, ▢, ▢
15. 39, 41, 43, ▢, ▢, ▢, ▢
16. 24, 22, 20, ▢, ▢, ▢, ▢
17. 37, 35, 33, ▢, ▢, ▢, ▢
18. 86, 88, 90, ▢, ▢, ▢, ▢
19. 98, 96, 94, ▢, ▢, ▢, ▢
20. 93, 91, 89, ▢, ▢, ▢, ▢
21. 74, 76, 78, ▢, ▢, ▢, ▢
22. 53, 51, 49, ▢, ▢, ▢, ▢
23. 44, 46, 48, ▢, ▢, ▢, ▢
24. 66, 64, 62, ▢, ▢, ▢, ▢
25. 47, 49, 51, ▢, ▢, ▢, ▢
26. 51, 49, 47, ▢, ▢, ▢, ▢
27. 35, 33, 31, ▢, ▢, ▢, ▢
28. 84, 82, 80, ▢, ▢, ▢, ▢
29. 95, 97, 99, ▢, ▢, ▢, ▢
30. 92, 94, 96, ▢, ▢, ▢, ▢

Challenge

Add together the numbers in each of these sequences.
   6, 8, 10, 12
   7, 9, 11, 13
   8, 10, 12, 14

What do you notice about the totals? Experiment with some sequences of your own.

Unit 3
Multiples

When we multiply two numbers together, the answer is called a **multiple**. 8 is a multiple of 2 and 4 because 2 × 4 = 8. All even numbers are multiples of 2. But only half of all even numbers are multiples of 4. Multiples of 10 end in 0. Multiples of 5 end in 5 or 0. Multiples of 50 end in 50 or 00. Below are numbers that are multiples of 2, 4, 5, 10 and 50. Write which of these number(s) they are multiples of.

Example 16 is a multiple of **2** and **4**

1. 6 is a multiple of
2. 15 is a multiple of
3. 4 is a multiple of and
4. 16 is a multiple of and
5. 30 is a multiple of and
6. 100 is a multiple of and
7. 10 is a multiple of and
8. 60 is a multiple of and
9. 35 is a multiple of
10. 88 is a multiple of and
11. 95 is a multiple of
12. 45 is a multiple of
13. 90 is a multiple of and
14. 14 is a multiple of
15. 900 is a multiple of and
16. 32 is a multiple of and
17. 75 is a multiple of
18. 180 is a multiple of and
19. 750 is a multiple of and
20. 150 is a multiple of and
21. 44 is a multiple of and
22. 160 is a multiple of and
23. 85 is a multiple of
24. 400 is a multiple of and
25. 56 is a multiple of and
26. 50 is a multiple of and
27. 270 is a multiple of and
28. 82 is a multiple of
29. 76 is a multiple of and
30. 700 is a multiple of and

Challenge

With a partner, make up a set of rules to decide if one number is a multiple of another.

When you have a set of rules, pick some numbers and test if they are multiples. You could check if you are correct by using a calculator – divide the number by 2, 4, 5, and 10.

Unit 4
Problems 1

1. Sara has six dishes and a bag of sweets. She puts one in the first dish, two in the second, three in the next and so on. How many sweets will she need for all the dishes?

2. She starts all over again, but this time she puts two sweets in the first dish, double that many in the second, double that into the next and so on. How many sweets will she need now?

3. Liam has 100 marbles to share equally among some friends. How many will they each get if he chooses
   (a) 10 friends
   (b) 5 friends
   (c) 4 friends
   (d) 50 friends
   (e) just 2 friends?

4. He decides to keep half for himself and share the rest between ten friends. How many does each friend get?

5. Kusum and Khalid are delivering papers on opposite sides of the same street. Kusum does the odd number side and goes to houses 3 to 21. Khalid delivers on the even side and goes to numbers 8 to 22.

   (a) How many papers does Kusum deliver?
   (b) How many papers does Khalid deliver?
   (c) How many papers do they need altogether?

6. Two giants run up a flight of 200 stairs. Amit the Giant goes up four steps at a time, but Giant Jack can manage five at a time.
   (a) How many strides does it take each of them?
   (b) How many more steps does one giant have to take than the other?

7. Coming back down the stairs, Amit shows off and jumps down five at a time. He falls down the last 20 steps. How many jumps did he make before falling?

8. Meena and Hayley have coins of each value and they share them. Meena chooses the coins with odd numbers, and Hayley has the coins with even numbers.
   (a) Which coins do they each have?
   (b) What is the total value of Meena's and Hayley's coins?

9. Simon eats Smarties ten at a time, but Yoshi eats them in fours. How many mouthfuls will it take each of them to eat 100 Smarties?

Unit 5
Place Value

The **place** of a digit in a number affects its **value**. The **5** in 3**3**5 has a value of **5**. The **5** in **2**50 has a value of **50**. The **5** in **3**576 has a value of **500**. The **5** in **5**382 has a value of **5000**. Write the value of the digit that is in bold print.

Example   2**3**5 30   4**8**23 800

1. 2**7**
2. **3**22
3. **4**8
4. **5**3
5. 3**1**55
6. 4**3**21
7. 3**2**2
8. **5**214
9. 5**3**5
10. 20**2**4
11. **2**024
12. 52**1**4
13. 72**5**0
14. 111**0**
15. 1**6**9
16. 29**6**5
17. 7**2**50
18. **3**965
19. **1**69
20. 2**0**24
21. 999**9**
22. **7**250
23. 2**9**65
24. 11**1**0
25. 432**1**
26. 169**4**
27. 1**6**94
28. 3**9**65
29. **2**70
30. 7**2**50

Challenge

How much difference does a place make?
Start with the number 1111.
(a) Subtract one digit at a time from 1111 to make four more numbers like this:
   1111 − 1 =   1111 − 10 =   1111 − 100 =   1111 − 1000 =
(b) Now subtract the smallest new number from the largest and put a ring around the answer.
(c) Do (a) and (b) again, starting with 2222, 3333 and 4444, for example 2222 − 2, and so on.
Look at the four starting numbers and the ringed answers. Can you see a pattern? What ringed answer will you get if you start with 5555?
Try with 5555, 6666, 7777, 8888 and 9999.

Unit 6
Number Sequences

Copy the numbers below, putting in the numbers between that are missing.

Example   335   340   335, **336, 337, 338, 339,** 340
              4761 4766 4761, **4762, 4763, 4764, 4765,** 4766
              228   223   228, **227, 226, 225, 224,** 223

1. 263 268
2. 852 857
3. 431 436
4. 2312 2317
5. 626 631
6. 437 432
7. 267 272
8. 4712 4719
9. 258 263
10. 1826 1821
11. 741 735
12. 139 144
13. 263 258
14. 2750 2755
15. 2317 2312
16. 7492 7487
17. 396 401
18. 6798 6803
19. 303 298
20. 657 662
21. 4905 4900
22. 4000 3995
23. 388 393
24. 998 1003
25. 502 497
26. 302 297
27. 2002 1997
28. 6999 7004
29. 2949 2954
30. 5071 5066

Challenge

Take a three-digit number (do not use 0). How many new numbers can you make by rearranging the digits?
Does it make a difference if two of the digits are the same?

Try the same with some four-digit numbers. What difference does it make when you have an extra digit?
What difference does it make when two or three digits are the same?

Unit 7
Number Ordering

Write these sets of numbers in order of size, either smallest to largest < or largest to smallest >.

Example > 263, 1622, 98, 684   1622, 684, 263, 98
< 734, 56, 7263, 64   56, 64, 734, 7263

1 < 567, 94, 2764, 443
2 > 67, 563, 86, 463
3 < 4856, 64, 754, 43
4 < 11, 18, 21, 19, 91, 12
5 < 53, 74, 46, 52, 87
6 > 9, 75, 6435, 37, 6
7 > 322, 319, 853, 333
8 > 2854, 654, 37, 736
9 < 6384, 3843, 342, 973
10 < 765, 46, 9, 456, 342
11 < 2, 2222, 222, 22, 23
12 > 45, 63, 37, 27, 38, 93
13 > 313, 3133, 333, 3313
14 > 567, 94, 2764, 443
15 < 463, 428, 429, 453, 46
16 < 87, 645, 324, 49, 495
17 > 11, 18, 21, 19, 91, 12
18 < 382, 3843, 38, 3884
19 > 2, 2222, 222, 22, 23
20 > 765, 46, 9, 456, 342
21 > 53, 74, 46, 52, 87
22 < 9, 75, 6435, 37, 6
23 > 463, 428, 429, 453, 46
24 < 1001, 101, 111, 1111
25 > 6384, 3843, 342, 973
26 < 45, 63, 37, 27, 38, 93
27 < 313, 3133, 333, 3313
28 < 6934, 696, 6943, 695
29 > 1001, 101, 111, 1111
30 > 87, 645, 324, 49, 495

Challenge

List the dates of birth of the children in your group or class in date order. Rearrange them according to the number of the day in the month, starting with the smallest number, then starting with the largest.

Do the same with the house numbers of the group.

Collect other sets of numbers, and do the same with them. Here are some ideas, but you can think of your own:
- number of children in each class
- number of boys in each class
- number of girls in each class.

Unit 8
Calculating with Multiples of 10

You can usually add or take away 1, 10, 100 or 1000 by simply adding or subtracting 1 from the correct column. This is because the place of the digit decides its value. Complete the equations below by adding or subtracting 1 from the correct column.

Example   3648 + 10 = 3658   3648 + 100 = 3748   3648 + 1000 = 4648

1. 272 + 10 =
2. 623 − 10 =
3. 735 + 1 =
4. 3852 − 100 =
5. 273 − 1 =
6. 2739 + 100 =
7. 3723 − 1000 =
8. 7462 + 100 =
9. 2994 + 1000 =
10. 2620 + 100 =
11. 9028 − 10 =
12. 9999 − 1 =
13. 2700 + 1 =
14. 6126 − 100 =
15. 2054 + 10 =
16. 6805 + 1000 =
17. 1617 − 10 =
18. 504 − 100 =
19. 8537 − 100 =
20. 531 − 1 =
21. 7083 + 1 =
22. 6386 − 1 =
23. 412 + 10 =
24. 9263 − 1000 =
25. 3903 + 10 =
26. 8059 + 1000 =
27. 2880 − 10 =
28. 3754 − 1000 =
29. 478 + 1 =
30. 5107 + 100 =

Challenge

Write down a four-digit number without using zero (0). Now add on and subtract the numbers below like this:

starting number 2845   + 100 = 2945, − 10 = 2935, + 1000 = 3935

starting number ....   + 1000 =   , − 100 =   , − 1 =   , + 10 =   , − 1000 =

Keep on adding or taking away 1, 10, 100 or 1000 until you get back to the number you started with.

Unit 9
Rounding to 10 and 100

Sometimes we only need to work to the nearest ten. On the number line, 27 is nearer to 30 than to 20, so we 'round it up' to **30**. If a digit is less than 5, we round down. If it is 5 or more, we round up.

0 1 2 3 4 5 6 7 8 9 **10** 11 12 13 14 15 16 17 18 19 **20** 21 22 23 24 25 26 27 28 29 **30** 31 32 33 34 35 36 37 38 39 **40**

Round the numbers below to the nearest ten.

1 44
2 8
3 49
4 32
5 19
6 53
7 74
8 93
9 78
10 46
11 31
12 65
13 23
14 36
15 30

Now round the following numbers to the nearest hundred.
If the number has fewer than 5 tens, round it down. If it has 5 or more tens, round it up.

Example   339 … **300**   274 … **300**   750 … **800**   542 … **500**

16 394
17 473
18 544
19 832
20 733
21 934
22 286
23 651
24 496
25 243
26 838
27 605
28 847
29 76
30 452

Challenge

Find out how many boys, girls and children altogether there are in your class.
Round each number to the nearest ten.
Total up the exact numbers and the rounded numbers – how close are they?

Find the total numbers of boys, girls and children altogether in your school and round them to the nearest hundred. How close are the rounded numbers and the real numbers?

Unit 10
Rounding to 1000

Sometimes we only need to work to the nearest whole number of thousands. If a number has fewer than five hundreds in the hundreds column, we round it down to the number of thousands. If a number has five or more hundreds in the hundreds column, we round up to the next thousand.

Round these numbers to the nearest thousand.
Put in an up ↑ or down ↓ arrow to show which way you have rounded.

Example   694 ...↑1000   3472 ...↓3000   7600 ...↑8000

1 684
2 1294
3 2094
4 9373
5 7449
6 4503
7 3747
8 8550
9 2943
10 2823

11 3537
12 3793
13 723
14 8274
15 4499
16 845
17 1945
18 3511
19 3744
20 1999

21 4634
22 6330
23 4391
24 7549
25 3943
26 8364
27 6357
28 8521
29 4937
30 5433

Challenge

Add together your rounded answers to questions 1, 2 and 3.
Use a calculator to total up the unrounded numbers for 1, 2 and 3.

Use the calculator to see how close the rounded and unrounded totals are.

Do the same with the other sets of three answers: 4, 5 and 6; 7, 8 and 9; and so on up to 28, 29 and 30.

Unit 11
Problems 2

For every 300 tokens collected, the school can claim a free book. Each class staples its tokens together in bundles of ten, and puts ten bundles into every envelope.

1. How many tokens would be in
   (a) 4 envelopes (b) 8 envelopes
   (c) 10 envelopes?

2. How many filled envelopes will they need for
   (a) 1 book (b) 10 books
   (c) 100 books?

After one week, this is what each class has collected:

Class 1   4 envelopes, 6 bundles, 7 loose tokens
Class 2   3 envelopes, 2 bundles, 4 loose tokens
Class 3   7 envelopes, 1 bundle, 3 loose tokens
Class 4   6 envelopes, 9 bundles, 2 loose tokens
Class 5   5 envelopes, 8 bundles, 6 loose tokens
Class 6   9 envelopes, 4 bundles, 1 loose token

3. (a) How many tokens altogether does each class have?
   (b) List the classes and their totals in order, starting with the largest number of tokens.

4. (a) What is each class's total rounded to the nearest 100?
   (b) Add up the 'rounded' class totals to get an estimated total for all the classes.

5. (a) Use a calculator to add up the exact total of tokens for all the classes.
   (b) How close is the estimated (rounded) total to the exact number?

Class 6 are given the job of sorting out all of the tokens.

6. (a) How many envelopes do they collect from the six classes?
   (b) How many bundles of ten do they collect from the classes?
   (c) How many loose tokens do they collect?

They put the loose tokens into bundles, and sort the loose bundles into envelopes of ten.

7. (a) How many envelopes do they have now?
   (b) How many loose bundles do they have now?
   (c) How many loose tokens do they have now?

8. How many books can they claim?

9. How many tokens do they have left over?

10. How many more tokens do they need to get another book?

Unit 12
Fractions

When we divide something into equal parts and keep one part, we write it like this:

$\frac{1}{3}$ one third $\frac{1}{4}$ one quarter

The number below the line is the number of equal parts.
If we have more than one of the equal parts, we write the fraction like this:

$\frac{2}{3}$ two thirds $\frac{3}{4}$ three quarters

Copy these fractions and write in words what they show.

Example $\frac{2}{5}$ = two fifths $\frac{7}{10}$ = seven tenths

1. $\frac{1}{2}$
2. $\frac{1}{4}$
3. $\frac{3}{5}$
4. $\frac{1}{10}$
5. $\frac{4}{8}$
6. $\frac{6}{10}$
7. $\frac{2}{3}$
8. $\frac{5}{8}$
9. $\frac{4}{6}$
10. $\frac{3}{4}$

If you double both the number of equal parts and number you have, you still have the same amount.

$\frac{1}{2} = \frac{2}{4}$ (×2) $\frac{2}{5} = \frac{4}{10}$ (×2) $\frac{3}{5} = \frac{9}{15}$ (×3) $\frac{2}{3} = \frac{8}{12}$ (×4)

It only works if you multiply the top and bottom by the same number. These are called **equivalent fractions**.

Fill in the spaces below to make pairs of equivalent fractions.

11. $\frac{1}{2} = \frac{3}{}$
12. $\frac{2}{3} = \frac{6}{}$
13. $\frac{1}{4} = \frac{}{8}$
14. $\frac{1}{5} = \frac{}{10}$
15. $\frac{3}{6} = \frac{6}{}$

16. $\frac{1}{3} = \frac{3}{}$
17. $\frac{4}{5} = \frac{8}{}$
18. $\frac{3}{4} = \frac{6}{}$
19. $\frac{1}{4} = \frac{}{8}$
20. $\frac{2}{3} = \frac{4}{}$

21. $\frac{1}{2} = \frac{}{6}$
22. $\frac{1}{2} = \frac{4}{}$
23. $\frac{1}{5} = \frac{2}{}$
24. $\frac{2}{3} = \frac{4}{}$
25. $\frac{3}{5} = \frac{6}{}$

26. $\frac{2}{} = \frac{4}{10}$
27. $\frac{1}{6} = \frac{2}{}$
28. $\frac{1}{} = \frac{3}{6}$
29. $\frac{1}{} = \frac{4}{8}$
30. $\frac{3}{} = \frac{6}{8}$

Challenge

Draw a 12 by 12 square on squared paper.
Colour one half blue, a quarter red, and two eighths yellow.

Unit 13
Comparing Fractions

Copy these pairs of fractions, putting one of these symbols in between.
= if the two fractions are equivalent (have the same value)
> if the first fraction is greater than the second
< if the first fraction is less than the second.

Example $\quad \frac{1}{2} = \frac{2}{4} \qquad \frac{3}{4} > \frac{1}{2} \qquad \frac{1}{4} < \frac{1}{3}$

1. $\frac{1}{2} \quad \frac{3}{4}$
2. $\frac{1}{4} \quad \frac{2}{4}$
3. $\frac{3}{5} \quad \frac{1}{2}$
4. $\frac{1}{8} \quad \frac{4}{8}$

5. $\frac{3}{8} \quad \frac{1}{2}$
6. $\frac{1}{2} \quad \frac{1}{4}$
7. $\frac{1}{5} \quad \frac{1}{4}$
8. $\frac{5}{10} \quad \frac{1}{2}$

9. $\frac{4}{6} \quad \frac{3}{6}$
10. $\frac{4}{6} \quad \frac{5}{6}$
11. $\frac{4}{8} \quad \frac{3}{4}$
12. $\frac{2}{10} \quad \frac{1}{5}$

13. $\frac{4}{8} \quad \frac{1}{2}$
14. $\frac{6}{10} \quad \frac{3}{5}$
15. $\frac{3}{6} \quad \frac{4}{8}$
16. $\frac{1}{2} \quad \frac{3}{5}$

17. $\frac{4}{5} \quad \frac{1}{2}$
18. $\frac{3}{4} \quad \frac{2}{3}$
19. $\frac{1}{4} \quad \frac{4}{5}$
20. $\frac{2}{3} \quad \frac{2}{5}$

Now put these fractions in order of size, starting with the smallest.

21. $\frac{4}{5} \quad \frac{2}{5} \quad \frac{1}{5}$
22. $\frac{1}{2} \quad \frac{1}{4} \quad \frac{3}{4}$

23. $\frac{1}{5} \quad \frac{3}{10} \quad \frac{1}{10}$
24. $\frac{2}{3} \quad \frac{1}{2} \quad \frac{1}{3}$

25. $\frac{3}{5} \quad \frac{3}{4} \quad \frac{3}{6}$
26. $\frac{2}{5} \quad \frac{2}{6} \quad \frac{2}{4}$

27. $\frac{1}{6} \quad \frac{2}{3} \quad \frac{3}{4}$
28. $\frac{1}{2} \quad \frac{1}{5} \quad \frac{2}{5}$

29. $\frac{4}{5} \quad \frac{1}{10} \quad \frac{1}{2}$
30. $\frac{3}{4} \quad \frac{4}{5} \quad \frac{2}{3}$

Challenge

Use a square piece of card or paper and draw diagonal lines from corner to corner.

Colour one half of the square and label it $\frac{1}{2}$.

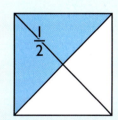

Colour one of the quarters in another colour and label it $\frac{1}{4}$.

Divide the remaining quarter into two eighths and colour and label one of them.
Divide the other eighth into sixteenths, colour and label one, and halve the other.
Keep going until the smallest fractions are too small to label.
Cut it up into triangles, then try to put it together again.

Unit 14
Finding Fractions

To find $\frac{1}{2}$ of a number, just divide it by **2**. $\frac{1}{2}$ of 8 is 4

To find $\frac{1}{3}$ of a number divide it by **3**. $\frac{1}{3}$ of 9 is 3

Find these fractions of the following numbers.

1. $\frac{1}{2}$ of 12
2. $\frac{1}{3}$ of 18
3. $\frac{1}{4}$ of 16
4. $\frac{1}{3}$ of 21
5. $\frac{1}{10}$ of 20
6. $\frac{1}{5}$ of 20
7. $\frac{1}{6}$ of 30
8. $\frac{1}{3}$ of 30
9. $\frac{1}{4}$ of 24
10. $\frac{1}{2}$ of 50

To find $\frac{3}{4}$ first find one quarter, then multiply the answer by 3.

$\frac{1}{4}$ of 16 is 4, so $\frac{3}{4}$ = 3 × 4 = 12

To find fifths, first find one fifth by dividing by 5, then multiply by 2 to get two fifths, or multiply by 3 to get three fifths, or by 4 to get four fifths. Do the same with these.

11. $\frac{2}{3}$ of 18
12. $\frac{3}{4}$ of 24
13. $\frac{2}{3}$ of 30
14. $\frac{5}{6}$ of 30
15. $\frac{2}{3}$ of 21
16. $\frac{3}{5}$ of 25
17. $\frac{7}{8}$ of 24
18. $\frac{3}{4}$ of 32
19. $\frac{3}{8}$ of 16
20. $\frac{5}{6}$ of 18
21. $\frac{2}{3}$ of 60
22. $\frac{3}{10}$ of 60
23. $\frac{4}{5}$ of 60
24. $\frac{3}{8}$ of 32
25. $\frac{7}{10}$ of 50
26. $\frac{3}{5}$ of 30
27. $\frac{3}{8}$ of 56
28. $\frac{7}{8}$ of 24
29. $\frac{5}{6}$ of 12
30. $\frac{9}{10}$ of 90

Challenge

On squared paper, draw a rectangle 12 squares wide and 10 squares deep.
Colour one tenth blue, two tenths green, one fifth yellow and one quarter red.
Colour the rest of the rectangle purple.
How many purple squares are there?
What fraction of the rectangle is purple?
Make up a similar challenge for a friend to try, **but make sure it works before giving the challenge!**

Unit 15
Problems 3

A school has 360 children. Work out how many children do each of the following:

1. (a) one quarter go to the library at least once a week
   (b) a quarter go sometimes but not as often
   (c) the rest do not go to the library at all!

2. (a) two ninths have read at least one Roald Dahl book
   (b) one third have read more than one book by him.

3. (a) three tenths like to play football at dinner time
   (b) one tenth think football is a silly game to play
   (c) one fifth prefer to play chasing games with their friends.

4. (a) three eighths bring packed lunches
   (b) one half stay for school dinners
   (c) the rest go home for dinner.

5. (a) seven eighths of the children say they would like homework
   (b) five eighths do homework.

6. (a) seven tenths think that their teachers are very old
   (b) a fifth believe their teachers when they say they're only 21 years old!

7. Last week one tenth were off ill, mostly with measles. How many came to school?

8. (a) two ninths walk to school alone
   (b) three fifths walk to school with someone else
   (c) the rest are driven to school.

9. (a) eleven twelfths would like to be rich and famous
   (b) one third would like to be a footballer
   (c) three quarters would like to be a pop star
   (d) two fifths can sing as badly as their favourite pop star.

10. (a) five sixths always put litter in the bin
    (b) one sixth drop litter on the floor
    (c) seven twelfths will tidy up a mess that someone else has made.

Unit 16
Addition and Subtraction

If we take a number away from another, then add it back again, we have what we started with.
$10 - 6 = 4$ then we can add it back $4 + 6 = 10$
This is because adding is the opposite of subtracting.
It works the other way round too.
$6 + 3 = 9$ take the 3 away $9 - 3 = 6$
Complete the following pairs of equations.

Examples $12 - 8 = 4$ so $4 + 8 = 12$ $15 - 7 = 8$ so $8 + 7 = 15$

1. $10 + 3 =$ ⬤ so ⬤ $- 3 = 10$
2. $9 - 4 =$ ⬤ so ⬤ $+ 4 = 9$
3. $15 + 4 =$ ⬤ so ⬤ $- 4 = 15$
4. $10 - 3 =$ ⬤ so ⬤ $+ 3 = 10$
5. $7 + 6 =$ ⬤ so ⬤ $- 6 = 7$
6. $12 - 4 =$ ⬤ so ⬤ $+ 4 = 12$
7. $9 + 5 =$ ⬤ so ⬤ $- 5 = 9$
8. $14 - 6 =$ ⬤ so ⬤ $+ 6 = 14$
9. $16 + 5 =$ ⬤ so ⬤ $- 5 = 16$
10. $16 - 6 =$ ⬤ so ⬤ $+ 6 = 16$
11. $15 - 3 =$ ⬤ so ⬤ $+ 3 = 15$
12. $14 + 3 =$ ⬤ so ⬤ $- 3 = 14$
13. $11 + 8 =$ ⬤ so ⬤ $- 8 = 11$
14. $2 + 9 =$ ⬤ so ⬤ $- 9 = 2$
15. $18 - 7 =$ ⬤ so ⬤ $+ 7 = 18$

16. $20 - 5 =$ ⬤ so ⬤ $+ 5 = 20$
17. $9 + 8 =$ ⬤ so ⬤ $- 9 = 8$
18. $8 + 6 =$ ⬤ so ⬤ $- 6 = 8$
19. $13 + 5 =$ ⬤ so ⬤ $- 5 = 13$
20. $3 + 17 =$ ⬤ so ⬤ $- 17 = 3$
21. $22 - 6 =$ ⬤ so ⬤ $+ 6 = 22$
22. $30 - 20 =$ ⬤ so ⬤ $+ 20 = 30$
23. $25 - 14 =$ ⬤ so ⬤ $+ 14 = 25$
24. $19 - 11 =$ ⬤ so ⬤ $+ 11 = 19$
25. $6 + 12 =$ ⬤ so ⬤ $- 12 = 6$
26. $15 + 5 =$ ⬤ so ⬤ $- 5 = 15$
27. $17 - 9 =$ ⬤ so ⬤ $+ 9 = 17$
28. $5 + 13 =$ ⬤ so ⬤ $- 13 = 5$
29. $22 - 8 =$ ⬤ so ⬤ $+ 8 = 22$
30. $7 + 11 =$ ⬤ so ⬤ $- 11 = 7$

Challenge

Make a long snake of paired equations, increasing the number you add and subtract each time. Do it like this.

$4 + 2 = 6$ $6 - 2 = 4$ $4 + 3 = 7$ $7 - 3 = 4$ $4 + 4 = 8$ $8 - 4 = 4$

Make a few more. Perhaps these snakes could be called adders!

Unit 17
Addition and Subtraction Facts

Complete the following equations. Take care to look at the signs. Some are additions and some are subtractions.

1. $7 + 6 =$
2. $10 - 3 =$
3. $9 + 8 =$
4. $30 + 20 =$
5. $11 - 8 =$
6. $7 + 7 + 2 =$
7. $2 + 10 + 4 =$
8. $30 + 70 =$
9. $100 - 70 =$
10. $10 - 4 =$
11. $6 + 2 + 9 =$
12. $3 + 4 + 7 =$
13. $6 + 3 + 5 =$
14. $8 + 5 + 4 =$
15. $11 - 7 =$
16. $60 + 30 =$
17. $40 + 50 =$
18. $20 - 13 =$
19. $14 - 5 =$
20. $2 + 4 + 8 =$
21. $4 + 5 + 6 =$
22. $10 + 9 =$
23. $90 - 40 =$
24. $13 - 5 =$
25. $80 - 70 =$
26. $11 + 9 =$
27. $50 + 20 =$
28. $8 + 5 =$
29. $8 + 6 + 1 =$
30. $13 - 9 =$

Challenge

When you add three or more numbers, you can often make it easier by adding them in a different order.

$7 + 5 + 3 =$ You know $7 + 3 = 10$, and $10 + 5 = 15$

$6 + 8 + 5 + 4 + 2 =$ You know $6 + 4 = 10$, and you know $8 + 2 = 10$, $10 + 10 = 20$, so $20 + 5 = 25$

Make up some equations like these and complete them using your own quick method, showing your working.

Unit 18
Addition and Subtraction to 100

Copy the equations below, filling in the missing numbers. One easy way is to add on units to make the next multiple of ten, then count on in tens.

Example   37 + ⬤ = 100   37 + 3 = 40   40 + 60 = 100, so 37 + 63 = 100

There are easy ways to subtract from 100. Try taking away the tens and units separately. Another way is to 'round up' the number you subtract, then add back the extra you took off.

Example   100 – 48   100 – 50 = 50, but we've taken off 2 too many, so add back: 50 + 2 = 52

1. 27 + ⬤ = 100
2. 100 – 70 = ⬤
3. 69 + ⬤ = 100
4. 100 – 64 = ⬤
5. 100 – 38 = ⬤
6. 75 + ⬤ = 100
7. 45 + ⬤ = 100
8. 62 + ⬤ = 100
9. 100 – 27 = ⬤
10. 100 – 47 = ⬤
11. 100 – 86 = ⬤
12. 100 – 45 = ⬤
13. 100 – 79 = ⬤
14. 100 – 35 = ⬤
15. 19 + ⬤ = 100
16. 55 + ⬤ = 100
17. 38 + ⬤ = 100
18. 95 + ⬤ = 100
19. 100 – 15 = ⬤
20. 84 + ⬤ = 100
21. 100 – 67 = ⬤
22. 32 + ⬤ = 100
23. 100 – 43 = ⬤
24. 27 + ⬤ = 100
25. 100 – 24 = ⬤
26. 77 + ⬤ = 100
27. 100 – 52 = ⬤
28. 41 + ⬤ = 100
29. 100 – 53 = ⬤
30. 59 + ⬤ = 100

Challenge

With a partner, each write down on a piece of paper ten equations for adding to make 100, and 10 for subtracting from 100, without the answers.
Swap them over face down. On the count of three, turn over and complete the equations written by your partner. The one who gets most correct, or all correct in the shorter time, is the winner.
You will both have to check the answers!

Unit 19
Facts to 50, 60, 70, 80, 90

Copy the equations below, filling in the missing number. One easy way is to add on units to make the next multiple of ten, then count on in tens.

Example 37 + ◯ = 60   37 + 3 = 40   40 + 20 = 60, so 37 + 23 = 60

When subtracting try taking away the tens and units separately. Another way is to 'round up' the number you subtract, then add back the extra you took off.

Example 70 − 49   70 − 50 = 20, but we've taken off 1 too many, so add back: 20 + 1 = 21

1. 27 + ◯ = 50
2. 90 − 75 = ◯
3. 69 + ◯ = 90
4. 80 − 64 = ◯
5. 50 − 38 = ◯
6. 75 + ◯ = 90
7. 45 + ◯ = 70
8. 62 + ◯ = 90
9. 60 − 27 = ◯
10. 70 − 47 = ◯
11. 80 − 36 = ◯
12. 70 − 45 = ◯
13. 50 − 39 = ◯
14. 60 − 35 = ◯
15. 19 + ◯ = 60
16. 55 + ◯ = 60
17. 38 + ◯ = 50
18. 55 + ◯ = 80
19. 50 − 15 = ◯
20. 34 + ◯ = 60
21. 60 − 27 = ◯
22. 32 + ◯ = 70
23. 70 − 43 = ◯
24. 27 + ◯ = 70
25. 90 − 24 = ◯
26. 27 + ◯ = 50
27. 80 − 52 = ◯
28. 41 + ◯ = 80
29. 90 − 53 = ◯
30. 59 + ◯ = 80

Challenge

With a partner, each write down on a piece of paper (without answers).
- four equations for adding up to 50
- four adding up to 60
- four adding up to 70
- four adding up to 80
- four adding up to 90.

Swap them over face down. On the count of three, turn over and complete the equations written by your partner. The one who gets most correct, or all correct in the shorter time, is the winner. You will both have to check the answers! Try again using subtraction equations instead.

Unit 20
Problems 4

1. Aysha buys small dolls with her pocket money. She is hoping to have the complete set of 20. In March she bought the first four, in April another three, and in May five more.
   (a) How many has she bought so far?
   (b) How many more does she need to complete the set?
   (c) If she now buys four a month from June onwards, when will she complete the set?

2. Charlie the dog likes to collect sticks from the park. He brought home two on Monday, three on Tuesday, one on Wednesday, two on Thursday, three on Friday and six on Saturday.
   (a) How many sticks has he got in his collection?
   (b) Which half of the week was more successful for stick collecting?
   (c) How many more sticks does he need to fetch on Sunday to make his collection up to 20?

3. Dad is fed up with Charlie's collection (20 sticks) but doesn't want to upset him. He decides to throw away five sticks a day while Charlie is out.
   (a) How many days will it take to get rid of them all if Charlie doesn't bring any more?
   (b) How many days will it take to get rid of them if Charlie brings two more home every day?
   (c) How many days will it take to get rid of them if Charlie brings three more home every day?

4. Auntie saves her aluminium drinks cans for recycling. She has ten canned drinks a week. She squashes them so that 80 will fit into one bag.
   (a) How many will she collect in six weeks?
   (b) How long will it take to fill one bag?
   (c) How many bags will she need after 24 weeks?

5. The family gets through 30 packets of crisps a week.
   They buy bags of 20 packets from the supermarket.

   (a) How many bags do they need every two weeks?
   (b) If they bought ten bags of 24 packets, how long would they last?
   (c) How many bags of 20 packets would last as long as ten bags of 24?

Unit 21
Small Differences

If you are finding the difference between two numbers that are quite close, it is easier to start with the lower number and count up to the higher number, than to subtract the lower from the higher:

Example 483 − 477 = 478 [+1], 479 [+2], 480 [+3], 481 [+4], 482 [+5], 483 [+6], so 483 − 477 = **6**.

Find these differences by counting up from the lower number to the higher number.

1   459 − 452 =
2   937 − 934 =
3   645 − 643 =
4   268 − 260 =
5   536 − 432 =
6   744 − 741 =
7   343 − 336 =
8   572 − 565 =
9   815 − 807 =
10 199 − 191 =

11 781 − 774 =
12 692 − 687 =
13 433 − 424 =
14 967 − 962 =
15 864 − 859 =
16 1659 − 1653 =
17 3734 − 3730 =
18 4356 − 4352 =
19 2482 − 2476 =
20 4852 − 4847 =

21 3453 − 3444 =
22 7005 − 6998 =
23 3001 − 2995 =
24 6002 − 5995 =
25 8063 − 8057 =
26 4003 − 3996 =
27 9979 − 9972 =
28 7007 − 6993 =
29 6175 − 6164 =
30 5006 − 4997 =

Challenge

Work with a partner. Each make up ten subtractions. Make sure that the units numeral in the first number is smaller than in the second number. Time how long it takes your partner to answer them correctly. Whoever completes all ten correctly in the shorter time is the winner. Work out the answers mentally.

Unit 22
Five and a Bit

> Try this short cut. When adding a few numbers, break them up into multiples of 5 then add on the 'bits' left over.
>
> **Example**   To work out 47 + 8
>   Split 47 up into 45 + 2, and split 8 up into 5 + 3
>
>   45 + 2 + 5 + 3
>   50
>   5
>   50 + 5 = 55
>
> Remember to do these in your head.

1. 37 + 15 =
2. 24 + 18 =
3. 56 + 24 =
4. 41 + 19 =
5. 26 + 36 =
6. 68 + 16 =
7. 27 + 56 =
8. 32 + 36 =
9. 66 + 28 =
10. 81 + 18 =
11. 79 + 27 =
12. 37 + 25 =
13. 43 + 28 =
14. 32 + 47 =
15. 51 + 34 =
16. 33 + 39 =
17. 28 + 53 =
18. 31 + 47 =
19. 45 + 27 =
20. 62 + 29 =
21. 67 + 12 =
22. 49 + 44 =
23. 56 + 26 =
24. 34 + 32 =
25. 78 + 7 =
26. 53 + 17 =
27. 24 + 46 =
28. 23 + 66 =
29. 36 + 57 =
30. 64 + 26 =

Challenge

Write down five equations like the ones above, including the answers.
Use a pencil to mark how you worked it out using this short cut. Look at the example in the box above to help you.
Make a second copy without marking the short cuts. You will give this to your partner in a moment.
Get a partner to do some as well, but don't show each other until you are ready to start.
One of you then times how long it takes the other to write down the answers correctly, without working them out on paper.
Now swap over, timing how long it takes the other person to do their partner's equations correctly.
The winner is the one who completes them all correctly in the shorter time.

Unit 23
Adding Tens and Units

Try this short cut. A quick way of adding two-digit numbers in your head is to add the tens and units separately.

Example   36 + 47
Start with 36 and add on the four tens   36 + 40 = 76
then add on the seven units   76 + 7 = 83
Use this method to complete these equations, working out the answers in your head.

1   43 + 35 =
2   45 + 23 =
3   56 + 22 =
4   64 + 24 =
5   38 + 41 =
6   73 + 27 =
7   44 + 26 =
8   55 + 26 =
9   46 + 36 =
10 64 + 28 =

11 39 + 33 =
12 28 + 25 =
13 49 + 47 =
14 28 + 24 =
15 27 + 17 =
16 45 + 29 =
17 76 + 27 =
18 63 + 28 =
19 48 + 39 =
20 29 + 18 =

21 57 + 35 =
22 73 + 19 =
23 69 + 28 =
24 42 + 29 =
25 65 + 28 =
26 47 + 48 =
27 36 + 57 =
28 39 + 38 =
29 76 + 18 =
30 68 + 25 =

Challenge

Make up five equations using two-digit numbers like the ones above. Include the answers, which must be less than 100.

Get a partner to do the same.
Read out your equations slowly while your partner works out each answer mentally.
Make sure your partner gives the correct answer before you read the next equation.
Time how long it takes.
Now swap over, timing how long it takes you to do your partner's equations correctly.
The winner is the one who completes all five correctly in the shorter time.

Unit 24
Cheating with 10

When you have to add or subtract 8 or 9 units in your head, you can 'cheat' by adding or subtracting 10 and then correcting the error.

Example 46 + 8   Add 10 instead of 8   46 + 10 = 56
But you've added 2 too many, so take off 2   56 – 2 = **54**
54 – 9   Subtract 10 instead of 9   54 – 10 = 44
But you've subtracted 1 too many, so add 1 back   44 + 1 = **45**

Use this method to complete the equations below, in your head.

1 45 + 8 =   4 43 – 9 =   7 34 + 8 =   10 37 – 8 =   13 46 + 9 =
2 56 – 8 =   5 75 + 8 =   8 47 + 9 =   11 58 + 8 =   14 46 – 8 =
3 67 – 9 =   6 83 + 9 =   9 57 – 9 =   12 95 – 8 =   15 35 + 9 =

You can use this method with bigger numbers, rounding to the nearest multiple of ten.
36 + 29   Add 30 instead of 29   36 + 30 = 66
You have added 1 too many, so take 1 off your answer.   66 – 1 = **65**

16 46 + 29 =   19 85 – 58 =   22 57 – 39 =   25 57 + 29 =   28 53 – 18 =
17 97 – 49 =   20 25 + 59 =   23 65 – 28 =   26 64 – 29 =   29 53 + 18 =
18 35 + 38 =   21 76 – 48 =   24 54 + 28 =   27 43 + 39 =   30 75 – 59 =

Challenge

Make up five equations like the ones in questions 16 to 30. Include the answers, which must be less than 100.

Get a partner to do the same. Read out your equations slowly while your partner works out each answer mentally.

Make sure your partner gives the correct answer before you read the next equation.
Time how long it takes.
Now swap over, timing how long it takes you to do your partner's equations correctly.
The winner is the one who completes all five correctly in the shorter time.
Try again with a new set of equations, trying to improve on your time.

Unit 25
Near Doubles

You should already know some doubles without having to work them out. You can use this knowledge to add 'near doubles' in your head.
Example 7 + 8 is close to double 7 or 8, so double 7 and add 1 on, or double 8 and take 1 off.
Do these equations in your head using the 'near doubles' short cut.

1. 6 + 7 =
2. 4 + 5 =
3. 5 + 6 =
4. 11 + 12 =
5. 8 + 7 =
6. 9 + 8 =

The method works well with larger numbers. Just double one number and then correct the error.
Example 16 + 17   Double 16 to 32 then add 1   32 + 1 = 33
or double 17 to 34 and take 1 off   34 − 1 = 33
Use this way to work out the following equations **in your head**.

7. 18 + 17 =
8. 15 + 16 =
9. 25 + 26 =
10. 23 + 24 =
11. 34 + 35 =
12. 28 + 29 =
13. 45 + 46 =
14. 29 + 30 =
15. 48 + 49 =
16. 37 + 38 =
17. 41 + 42 =
18. 50 + 51 =
19. 59 + 60 =
20. 72 + 71 =
21. 62 + 61 =
22. 75 + 76 =
23. 160 + 161 =
24. 230 + 231 =

These are also easy. Think of them as a number of tens.
Example 230 + 240 is 23 tens + 24 tens, so double 24 to 48 and take 1 off
48 − 1 = 47   47 tens = **470**

25. 260 + 270 =
26. 320 + 330 =
27. 490 + 480 =
28. 370 + 380 =
29. 340 + 350 =
30. 450 + 460 =

Challenge

Make up a few problems that can be solved in your head using the 'near doubles' method.

Example There are 35 children in Year 3 and 36 in Year 4; how many are there altogether?

Swap with a friend and solve each other's.
Did you double the smaller number and add on, or double the larger one and take off?

Unit 26
Adding Several Numbers

Add up these sets of numbers in your head, using short cuts to make it easier. Possible short-cuts are: finding pairs of numbers that add up to 10, splitting the units up to round up to the next multiple of 10, adding the tens and units separately, using 'near multiples' of 10 and using 'near doubles'.

1. 5, 9, 6
2. 14, 4, 15
3. 25, 7, 26
4. 4, 9, 6, 2
5. 13, 14, 15, 16
6. 22, 25, 23, 12
7. 6, 8, 24, 9
8. 53, 29, 8
9. 23, 31, 43
10. 25, 8, 5, 4
11. 24, 8, 9, 19
12. 5, 13, 6, 7, 4
13. 38, 46, 14
14. 24, 12, 25
15. 32, 15, 33
16. 87, 6, 10
17. 17, 6, 13, 12
18. 19, 24, 18, 16
19. 22, 11, 28, 30
20. 2, 3, 4, 5, 6, 7, 8, 9
21. 8, 6, 32, 14, 7
22. 43, 34, 13
23. 13, 6, 12, 7, 9
24. 7, 8, 25, 19
25. 27, 33, 24, 12
26. 3, 8, 3, 2, 7
27. 28, 15, 27, 14
28. 14, 8, 8, 28
29. 15, 6, 35, 7
30. 21, 6, 19, 6, 10

Challenge

Copy down one of the sets of numbers.
Use different-coloured pencils to show the short cuts you could use.

Example

= 20 + 7   = 28 + 32 = 60   + 7

Try the same with a few more of the sets of numbers.
Compare the short cuts you used with the ones used by someone else.

Unit 27
Number Patterns

There is a pattern in each group of three equations below.

Finding and following the pattern will make the second and third equations easier to complete.

Example 35 + 26 = 61   35 + 36 = 71   35 + 46 = 81
                              + 10 more   + 10 more

1 45 + 22 =
2 45 + 32 =
3 45 + 42 =
4 28 + 64 =
5 28 + 54 =
6 28 + 44 =
7 23 + 37 =
8 33 + 37 =
9 43 + 37 =

10 54 + 41 =
11 54 + 31 =
12 54 + 21 =
13 18 + 19 =
14 18 + 39 =
15 18 + 59 =
16 74 + 17 =
17 64 + 17 =
18 54 + 17 =

19 18 + 62 =
20 18 + 42 =
21 18 + 22 =
22 87 + 12 =
23 67 + 12 =
24 47 + 12 =
25 43 + 40 =
26 33 + 45 =
27 43 + 50 =

Challenge

You need a number square (1 to 100).

Use a crayon and colour in the squares that have the answers to equations 1, 2 and 3 above.

Change colour and do the same with the answers to 4, 5 and 6.

Repeat this, changing colour each time, for the other equations.

Unit 28
Using Place Value 1

Work out these equations in your head.
Remember It is usually easier to start with the larger number first. The place of a digit in a number affects its value.
The 4 in 240 has a value of **4 tens, 40**; but in 439 it has a value of **4 hundreds, 400**. It is sometimes easier to use multiples: for example, 120 + 50 is **12** tens + **5** tens = **17** tens, **170**

1. 254 + 30 =
2. 168 − 40 =
3. 26 + 400 =
4. 60 + 90 =
5. 150 − 70 =
6. 800 + 700 =
7. 389 − 70 =
8. 600 + 300 =
9. 280 − 60 =
10. 230 − 60 =
11. 70 + 80 + 50 =
12. 565 + 200 =
13. 260 + 330 =
14. 172 − 40 =
15. 330 + 70 =
16. 687 − 250 =
17. 748 + 130 =
18. 100 − 45 =
19. 200 + 100 + 500 =
20. 200 − 149 =
21. 642 − 320 =
22. 2059 + 830 =
23. 1300 + 500 =
24. 240 + 160 =
25. 497 − 85 =
26. 70 − 46 =
27. 786 − 370 =
28. 800 − 455 =
29. 200 + 3780 =
30. 230 + 220 + 350 =

Challenge

Many short cuts can be used to add and subtract mentally.
Copy out five of the equations above, then use colouring pencils to show the short cuts you used to find the answer:

68 tens − 25 tens = **43 tens**

687 − 250   43 tens + 7 = **437**

7 − 0 = 7

- Adding or subtracting in multiples of 10 or 100, then correcting the error
  430 − 90   Take off 100 instead, then put 10 back
- Adding pairs of numbers that add up to 10
  3 + 5 + 7   Add the 3 + 7 first to make 10, then add on the remaining 5
- Adding doubles or near doubles
  80 + 80 = 160   80 + 79 = 159   49 + 50 = 99
- Working in multiples of 10 or 100
  700 + 800 is the same as 7 hundreds + 8 hundreds = 15 hundreds, 1500
- Adding or subtracting part of a number first to round up or down
  530 − 80   Subtract 30 first to round down to 500, then take off the remaining 50

Unit 29
Using Place Value 2

Work out these equations in your head.
Remember It is usually easier to start with the larger number first.
The place of a digit in a number affects its value.
The 4 in 240 has a value of **4 tens, 40**; but in 439 it has a value of **4 hundreds, 400**.
It is sometimes easier to use multiples:
    120 + 50 is **12** tens + **5** tens = **17** tens, **170**

1 225 + 50 =
2 198 − 37 =
3 206 + 400 =
4 606 + 80 =
5 450 − 60 =
6 700 + 650 =
7 394 − 72 =
8 470 + 330 =
9 420 − 80 =
10 530 − 140 =

11 62 + 70 + 40 =
12 734 + 240 =
13 390 + 430 =
14 152 − 41 =
15 2330 + 170 =
16 438 − 225 =
17 567 + 232 =
18 400 − 235 =
19 400 + 200 + 350 =
20 800 − 551 =

21 372 − 261 =
22 6559 + 800 =
23 3600 + 500 =
24 640 + 270 =
25 394 − 99 =
26 800 − 360 =
27 687 − 280 =
28 900 − 351 =
29 400 + 5390 =
30 140 + 320 + 210 =

Challenge

Many short cuts can be used to add and subtract mentally.
Copy out five of the equations above, then use
colouring pencils to show the short cuts you used to find the answer.
Here are some short cuts you might have used, but there are others:
- Adding or subtracting in multiples of 10 or 100, then correcting the error
  430 − 90   Take off 100 instead, then put 10 back
- Adding pairs of numbers that add up to 10
  3 + 5 + 7   Add the 3 + 7 first to make 10, then add on the remaining 5
- Adding doubles or near doubles
  80 + 80 = 160   80 + 79 = 159   49 + 50 = 99
- Working in multiples of 10 or 100
  700 + 800 is the same as 7 hundreds + 8 hundreds = 15 hundreds, 1500
- Adding or subtracting part of a number first to round up or down
  530 − 80   Subtract 30 first to round down to 500, then take off the remaining 50

Unit 30
Problems 5

1. Look at these cricket scores. Total the runs per team and say which team won and by how much.
   (a) Lancashire 1st innings 224, 2nd innings 351; Yorkshire 1st innings 256, 2nd innings 312
   (b) Surrey 1st innings 124, 2nd innings 230; Essex 1st innings 153, 2nd innings 202
   (c) Somerset 1st innings 325, 2nd innings 234; Kent 1st innings 199, 2nd innings 192.

2. A school kitchen asks children to order their dinners on a Monday for the rest of the week.
   Because children are sometimes away, the figures are usually 'out' (they don't match up).

	Mon	Tues	Wed	Thurs	Fri
Ordered	231	231	228	232	224
Bought	231	235	226	239	218

   (a) Find the weekly total for dinners ordered and dinners bought.
   (b) For each day, find out how much the numbers were 'out' – what was the error?
   (c) What was the total error for the whole week?

3. A family went caravan touring in Europe. When they left home, the car had gone 33 545 miles. When they returned, it had gone 35 496 miles.
   They towed the caravan 1353 miles.
   (a) How far did they drive altogether?
   (b) How far did they drive without the caravan?

4. Some children needed to swim 20 lengths each week to win a competition. Here's how they did:

   Becky 18, 19, 20, 19, 17
   Vivek 16, 15, 15, 14, 16
   Miho   12, 10, 11, 12, 13
   Sam   16, 17, 10, 19, 17

   (a) Add up their totals.
   (b) How many more did each child need?
   (c) How many more lengths did they need altogether?

Unit 31
Adding with Pencil and Paper 1

Copy and work out these additions in columns.
Use notes to help.

1. 146 + 32
2. 523 + 56
3. 361 + 42
4. 425 + 43
5. 374 + 51
6. 293 + 36
7. 435 + 38
8. 373 + 59
9. 157 + 39
10. 466 + 63
11. 345 + 76
12. 437 + 34
13. 354 + 65
14. 564 + 39
15. 745 + 55
16. 487 + 45
17. 625 + 49
18. 197 + 38
19. 365 + 267
20. 574 + 347
21. 395 + 483
22. 247 + 647
23. 482 + 348
24. 657 + 144
25. 236 + 642
26. 485 + 465
27. 173 + 757
28. 347 + 572
29. 375 + 386
30. 352 + 453

Challenge

Find the totals of the following, using your library or the internet:
(a) the number of days in a leap year and the number of weeks in a year
(b) the number of days in a non-leap year and the number of days in a lunar month
(c) the number of days in a non-leap year before your birthday and the number of days after
(d) the number of days in a non-leap year before your friend's birthday and the number of days after.

Unit 32
Adding with Pencil and Paper 2

Copy and work out these additions in columns. Use notes to help.

1	34 + 31 + 23	6	43 + 26 + 27	11	74 + 34 + 24	16	48 + 60 + 24	21	56 + 84 + 46	26	92 + 28 + 39
2	16 + 26 + 22	7	47 + 26 + 53	12	61 + 26 + 39	17	53 + 26 + 73	22	75 + 38 + 25	27	29 + 69 + 49
3	42 + 25 + 31	8	63 + 25 + 63	13	54 + 35 + 27	18	25 + 33 + 79	23	66 + 77 + 88	28	99 + 89 + 79
4	25 + 36 + 21	9	19 + 47 + 68	14	38 + 19 + 37	19	52 + 30 + 78	24	49 + 36 + 74	29	35 + 74 + 49
5	63 + 26 + 17	10	58 + 51 + 54	15	35 + 37 + 29	20	80 + 53 + 15	25	58 + 33 + 86	30	84 + 96 + 85

Challenge

1 How many days are there from:
   (a) January to March (in both leap and non-leap years)
   (b) April to June
   (c) July to September
   (d) October to December?

2 (a) Measure three people's cubits in centimetres (the length from their bent elbow to their fingertips).
   (b) Find the total length.
   (c) Try the same with three other people.

Unit 33
Subtracting with Pencil and Paper

Complete these subtractions.
Use notes to help.

1. 153 − 45
2. 265 − 57
3. 162 − 47
4. 356 − 61
5. 358 − 39
6. 186 − 34
7. 195 − 39
8. 498 − 37
9. 390 − 72
10. 293 − 94
11. 762 − 45
12. 381 − 79
13. 111 − 37
14. 116 − 52
15. 308 − 39
16. 596 − 444
17. 590 − 478
18. 676 − 451
19. 662 − 462
20. 740 − 637
21. 578 − 426
22. 992 − 316
23. 572 − 480
24. 458 − 239
25. 347 − 248
26. 722 − 629
27. 402 − 107
28. 365 − 296
29. 475 − 376
30. 802 − 123

Challenge

Subtract:
(a) the number of days in the year before your birthday from the number of days in a non-leap year
(b) the number of days in the year after your birthday from the number of days in a non-leap year.
Add together the two answers.
Do the same for a friend's birthday and again add together the two answers.
What do you notice?
Can you predict how many days will come after a birthday by looking at the number of days before?

Unit 34
Problems 6

Work out the answers to these problems in columns like this:

$$\begin{array}{r} 49 \\ +44 \\ \hline \end{array}$$

Show your working out as well as your answer.

Phil the dentist counts up how many fillings he does. When he has done 600, he is going to buy a new drill. Work out his weekly totals. It might be easier to add one day at a time.

Week 1   Mon. 15, Tues. 24, Wed. 18, Thurs. 22, Fri. 12
1 (a) How many fillings this week?
   (b) How many more does he need before he can buy that new drill?

Week 2   Mon. 23, Tues. 22, Wed. 20, Thurs. 19, Fri. 17
2 (a) How many fillings this week?
   (b) How many fillings in total so far?
   (c) How many more does he need now to buy that new drill?

Week 3   Mon. 21, Tues. 18, Wed. 22, Thurs. 17, Fri. 16
3 (a) How many fillings this week?
   (b) How many fillings in total so far?
   (c) How many more does he need now to buy that new drill?

Week 4 is 'Children in Need' week. Phil was sponsored £1·50 for every filling done.
              Mon. 53, Tues. 62, Wed. 45, Thurs. 56, Fri. 87
4 (a) How many fillings this week?
   (b) How many fillings for the four weeks altogether?
   (c) How many more does he need now to buy that new drill?
   (d) How much did he raise for 'Children in Need'?

In week 5, 126 of the week 4 patients complain that their new fillings have fallen out. 36 of them go to a new dentist; the rest agree for him to do the job again, more carefully.
5 (a) How many week 4 patients did not complain?
   (b) How many fillings does Phil refill?
   (c) How long will it take him to do them if he does 30 a day?

"Phil the Drill"
Teeth repairs by an expert
Try our 'while you wait' service

To get new patients, he advertises.
The advertisement costs £36 a week or £100 for four weeks.
6 (a) What would it cost for four separate weeks?
   (b) How much would Phil save if he bought the '£100 for 4 weeks' offer?

Unit 35
Multiplication and Division

When we multiply a number by 3, we make it three times bigger. $4 \times 3 = 12$
When we divide a number by 3, we make it three times smaller. $12 \div 3 = 4$
Multiplication and division are **inverse operations** – they do the opposite of each other.
We can undo a multiplication by dividing the answer like this. $6 \times 7 = 42, 42 \div 7 = 6$
We can undo a division by multiplying the answer like this. $16 \div 2 = 8, 8 \times 2 = 16$
Doubling (×2) and **halving** (÷2) are also **inverse operations** – they do the opposite.
Complete these pairs of inverse operations by filling in the missing number.

Example $5 \times 6 = 30$ $30 \div 6 = 5$ $48 \div 8 = 6$ $6 \times 8 = 48$

1. $4 \times 5 =$ ◯   ◯ $\div 5 = 4$
2. $36 \div 4 =$ ◯   ◯ $\times 4 = 36$
3. $6 \times 9 =$ ◯   ◯ $\div 9 = 6$
4. $27 \div 3 =$ ◯   ◯ $\times 3 = 27$
5. $3 \times 7 =$ ◯   ◯ $\div 7 = 3$
6. $56 \div 7 =$ ◯   ◯ $\times 7 = 56$
7. $8 \times 3 =$ ◯   ◯ $\div 3 = 8$
8. $24 \div 6 =$ ◯   ◯ $\times 6 = 24$
9. $4 \times 4 =$ ◯   ◯ $\div 4 = 4$
10. $36 \div 9 =$ ◯   ◯ $\times 9 = 36$
11. $7 \times 5 =$ ◯   ◯ $\div 5 = 7$
12. $72 \div 8 =$ ◯   ◯ $\times 8 = 72$
13. $9 \times 8 =$ ◯   ◯ $\div 8 = 9$
14. $30 \div 5 =$ ◯   ◯ $\times 5 = 30$
15. $10 \times 6 =$ ◯   ◯ $\div 6 = 10$
16. $63 \div 9 =$ ◯   ◯ $\times 9 = 63$
17. $5 \times 9 =$ ◯   ◯ $\div 9 = 5$
18. $54 \div 6 =$ ◯   ◯ $\times 6 = 54$
19. $6 \times 6 =$ ◯   ◯ $\div 6 = 6$
20. $56 \div 8 =$ ◯   ◯ $\times 8 = 56$
21. $20 \div 4 =$ ◯   ◯ $\times 4 = 20$
22. $24 \div 8 =$ ◯   ◯ $\times 8 = 24$
23. $4 \times 8 =$ ◯   ◯ $\div 8 = 4$
24. $28 \div 4 =$ ◯   ◯ $\times 4 = 28$
25. $3 \times 6 =$ ◯   ◯ $\div 6 = 3$
26. $15 \div 3 =$ ◯   ◯ $\times 3 = 15$
27. $7 \times 8 =$ ◯   ◯ $\div 8 = 7$
28. $54 \div 9 =$ ◯   ◯ $\times 9 = 54$
29. $9 \times 3 =$ ◯   ◯ $\div 3 = 9$
30. $9 \times 4 =$ ◯   ◯ $\div 4 = 9$

Challenge

Start with 12 cubes and arrange them in three rows of four to make a cuboid one cube deep.
Draw the top face of the cuboid like this. $3 \times 4 = 12$
Separate the rows slightly and draw and label them again. $12 \div 3 = 4$
Repeat using the 12 cubes in other rectangular shapes.
Repeat using 36, 40, 48 and 60 cubes.

Unit 36
Remainders and Rounding

If we divided 9 cubes by 2, we would have two sets of 4 plus 1 cube left over. The leftover cube is called the **remainder**.
We write it like this. $9 \div 2 = 4 \text{ r } 1$

Complete these division equations, writing in the remainder.

1. $13 \div 3 =$
2. $36 \div 8 =$
3. $25 \div 4 =$
4. $23 \div 4 =$
5. $43 \div 10 =$
6. $46 \div 6 =$
7. $30 \div 9 =$
8. $34 \div 5 =$
9. $29 \div 3 =$
10. $17 \div 5 =$
11. $53 \div 7 =$
12. $35 \div 6 =$
13. $66 \div 7 =$
14. $42 \div 9 =$
15. $63 \div 8 =$

If we have a remainder when we divide objects or money, we have to decide if we should round up or down.

Example How many 3p sweets can you buy for 10p?
You can buy 3 sweets with 1p left over.
How many 4-seater tables do we need for 23 children? We need 6 tables, 1 table will have an empty space.

Complete the following divisions. Write your answers like these examples.

16. How many 8p cakes can you buy for 30p?
17. How many 12-seater mini-buses are needed for 40 children?
18. How many £6 books can you buy with £35?
19. If 6 eggs fit in a box, how many boxes are needed for 27 eggs?
20. How many £9 football match tickets can you buy for £50?
21. From a jar of 100 sweets, how many children can have 9 sweets?
22. How many 6-packs of lollies are needed for a class of 28?
23. How many 10p sweets can you buy for 75p?
24. If 5 cakes fit in a box, how many boxes are needed for 24?
25. How many 52-seater coaches are needed for 130 children?
26. How many £1·20 burgers can you buy for £4·27?
27. How many 12-packs of pencils are needed for a class of 28?
28. A garage has 15 new tyres. How many cars can have 4?
29. How many 24-packs of books are needed for a class of 28?
30. How many 18p stamps can you buy for 50p?

Challenge
Make up some rounding up and rounding down division stories of your own.

Unit 37
Problems 7

The SafeCo Supermarket is giving away vouchers for schools to collect for free computer equipment. They will give customers one voucher for every £20 they spend. Schools can exchange:

180 vouchers for a printer
35 vouchers for a CD-ROM
900 vouchers for a computer
90 vouchers for a scanner
300 vouchers for a digital camera
10 vouchers for a pack of 12 floppy disks.

1 (a) How many computers could a school get with 1000 vouchers?
   (b) How many vouchers would they have left over?

2 (a) How many digital cameras could they get with 1000 vouchers?
   (b) How many vouchers would they have left over?

3 (a) How many scanners could they get with 1000 vouchers?
   (b) How many vouchers would they have left over?

4 (a) How many CD-ROMs could they get with 1000 vouchers?
   (b) How many vouchers would they have left over?

5 (a) How many floppy disks could they get with 1000 vouchers?
   (b) How many vouchers would they have left over?

These schools have collected a number of vouchers. 'Spend' as many of their vouchers as you can.

6 Billinge School has collected 530 vouchers.
   (a) What could they buy?
   (b) How many vouchers would they have left over?

7 Priory School has collected 949 vouchers.
   (a) What could they buy?
   (b) How many vouchers would they have left over?

8 The Rowland School has collected 1489 vouchers.
   (a) What could they buy?
   (b) How many vouchers would they have left over?

Unit 38

Multiplying by 2, 5 and 10

Complete the following. If you know your 2, 5 and 10 times tables, you should be able to get all of them correct in just a few minutes.
If you have to work out the answers, you don't know your tables.
Knowing your tables means having the answers already in your head.

1 3 × 2 =
2 9 × 5 =
3 4 × 10 =
4 6 × 5 =
5 ☐ × 2 = 6
6 5 × 2 =
7 8 × ☐ = 16
8 6 × 10 =
9 ☐ × 5 = 25
10 ☐ × 10 = 90

11 4 × 2 =
12 7 × 10 =
13 6 × 2 =
14 ☐ × 2 = 18
15 4 × 5 =
16 3 × 10 =
17 10 × 5 =
18 ☐ × 10 = 40
19 8 × 2 =
20 7 × 2 =

21 8 × 5 =
22 ☐ × 5 = 40
23 3 × 5 =
24 ☐ × 2 = 12
25 10 × 2 =
26 ☐ × 5 = 45
27 9 × 2 =
28 8 × 10 =
29 7 × 5 =
30 ☐ × 10 = 30

Challenge

Copy out the equations above, but turn the numbers around the other way like this.

3 × 2 = ☐ → 2 × 3 = ☐

☐ × 2 = 18 → 2 × ☐ = 18

Now get a friend to time you while you write in the answers. What have you noticed about the answers?

Now turn them around this way:

3 × 2 = ☐ → ☐ × 2 = 6

☐ × 2 = 18 → 9 × 2 = ☐

Get your friend to test you again. Try to improve your time.

Unit 39
Multiplying by 3, 4, 6 and 8

Complete the following. If you know your 3 and 4 times tables, you should be able to get all of them correct in just a few minutes. If you have to work out the answers, you don't know your tables. Knowing your tables means having the answers already in your head.

1 $2 \times 3 =$
2 $7 \times 3 =$
3 $2 \times 4 =$
4 $3 \times 3 =$
5 $8 \times 4 =$
6 $4 \times 3 =$

7 $7 \times 4 =$
8 $9 \times 3 =$
9 $8 \times 3 =$
10 $3 \times 4 =$
11 $10 \times 4 =$
12 $5 \times 4 =$

13 $6 \times 3 =$
14 $9 \times 4 =$
15 $6 \times 4 =$
16 $5 \times 3 =$
17 $10 \times 3 =$
18 $4 \times 4 =$

If you know your 3 and 4 times tables, you can do 6 and 8 times by 'doubling up'.
6 is double 3, so $4 \times 3 = 12$ will double up to $4 \times 6 = 24$
8 is double 4, so $2 \times 4 = 8$ will double up to $2 \times 8 = 16$
Use this doubling up method to complete these equations.

19 $2 \times 6 =$
20 $7 \times 6 =$
21 $3 \times 8 =$
22 $3 \times 6 =$

23 $4 \times 8 =$
24 $8 \times 6 =$
25 $7 \times 8 =$
26 $4 \times 6 =$

27 $5 \times 8 =$
28 $5 \times 6 =$
29 $9 \times 8 =$
30 $6 \times 8 =$

Challenge

Copy out all the equations above, but turn the numbers around the other way like this:
$7 \times 3 =$ → $3 \times 7 =$

Get a friend to time you while you fill in the answers.
Now that you 'know' the answers, rearrange them to look like this, leaving a space at the start:
$7 \times 3 =$ → $\times 3 = 21$

Get your friend to time you again. Try to improve on your time.

Unit 40
Dividing by 2, 5 and 10

Complete the following. If you know your 2, 5 and 10 times tables, you should be able to get all of them correct in just a few minutes.
If you have to work out the answers, you don't know your tables. Knowing your tables means having the answers already in your head.

1 40 ÷ 5 =
2 12 ÷ 2 =
3 70 ÷ 10 =
4 60 ÷ 10 =
5 50 ÷ 5 =
6 10 ÷ 2 =
7 4 ÷ 2 =
8 14 ÷ 2 =
9 5 ÷ 5 =
10 100 ÷ 10 =

11 20 ÷ 10 =
12 35 ÷ 5 =
13 20 ÷ 2 =
14 25 ÷ 5 =
15 2 ÷ 2 =
16 50 ÷ 10 =
17 10 ÷ 10 =
18 15 ÷ 5 =
19 8 ÷ 2 =
20 18 ÷ 2 =

21 40 ÷ 10 =
22 20 ÷ 5 =
23 90 ÷ 10 =
24 6 ÷ 2 =
25 16 ÷ 2 =
26 45 ÷ 5 =
27 80 ÷ 10 =
28 10 ÷ 5 =
29 30 ÷ 10 =
30 30 ÷ 5 =

Challenge

You need a number square (1 to 100).
Use one colour of crayon to colour each square containing a number that is a multiple of 5 (5, 10, 15 and so on).
If the number is also an even number, only colour half of it. Save the other half for the next stage.
Use a different colour to colour the even numbers.
If the number is also a multiple of 5, there should only be half a square left for you to colour.
Study the finished pattern. What does it show?

7	8	9	10
17	18	19	20
27	28	29	30
37	38	39	40

Unit 41
Dividing by 3 and 4

Complete the following. If you know your 3 and 4 times tables, you should be able to get all of them correct in just a few minutes. If you have to work out the answers, you don't know your tables. Knowing your tables means having the answers already in your head.

1 40 ÷ 4 =
2 12 ÷ 3 =
3 ◯ ÷ 3 = 7
4 ◯ ÷ 4 = 6
5 16 ÷ 4 =
6 30 ÷ 3 =
7 3 ÷ 3 =
8 15 ÷ 3 =
9 4 ÷ 4 =
10 ◯ ÷ 3 = 5

11 27 ÷ 3 =
12 32 ÷ 4 =
13 21 ÷ 3 =
14 24 ÷ 4 =
15 6 ÷ 3 =
16 ◯ ÷ 3 = 10
17 ◯ ÷ 3 = 6
18 12 ÷ 4 =
19 18 ÷ 3 =
20 24 ÷ 3 =

21 ◯ ÷ 4 = 8
22 20 ÷ 4 =
23 ◯ ÷ 3 = 9
24 9 ÷ 3 =
25 ◯ ÷ 4 = 4
26 36 ÷ 4 =
27 ◯ ÷ 4 = 3
28 8 ÷ 4 =
29 ◯ ÷ 4 = 9
30 28 ÷ 4 =

Challenge

You need a number square (1 to 100). Use one colour of crayon to colour each square containing a number that is a multiple of 3 (3, 6, 9, 12, 15 and so on). **If the number is also a multiple of 4 (4, 8, 12, 16 and so on), only colour half of it. Save the other half for the next stage.** Use a different colour to colour the multiples of 4 (4, 8, 12 and so on). If the number is also a multiple of 3, there should only be half a square left for you to colour.

Study the finished pattern. What does it show?

1	2	3	4
11	12	13	14
21	22	23	24
31	32	33	34

Unit 42
Double Quick

This page is all about doubling numbers – multiplying numbers by 2. Below you are given a starting number. Double it to fill in the next space and carry on until you have run out of spaces.

Example   6 → 6, 12, 24, 48

1. 3,
2. 21
3. 19
4. 17
5. 25
6. 1
7. 5
8. 13,
9. 75
10. 11
11. 19
12. 15
13. 9
14. 85
15. 35,
16. 45,
17. 23
18. 7
19. 110
20. 65
21. 95

If you are doubling multiples of 10 or 50, remove the zero(s), do the doubling, then put the zero(s) back.

Example
20 → 2(0), 4(0), 8(0), 16(0), 32(0), 64(0) → 20, 40, 80, 160, 320, 640

22. 350
23. 250
24. 100
25. 300
26. 550
27. 650
28. 150
29. 270
30. 450

Challenge

You will need a number line or a 100 cm ruler (a metre stick marked with centimetres), and a few small items to use as markers (cm cubes, counters, buttons – anything small). If you use a number line on the wall, you will also need some Blu-tack. Place a marker by the number 1. Double the number and place another marker. Keep on doubling until you run out of ruler. Look at the positions of the markers. What is happening? Can you explain why? Repeat, starting with 3, 5, 7, 9 and 11. Does the same thing happen?

Unit 43
Quick Halves

This page is all about halving numbers – dividing a number by 2.

Below you are given a starting number.

Halve it and carry on halving until you reach an odd number.

Example   48, **24**, **12**, **6**, **3** (stop at 3 because it is an odd number)
100, **50**, **25** (stop at 25 because it is an odd number)

1 36
2 44
3 80
4 48
5 640
6 32
7 880
8 42
9 900
10 68

11 92
12 52
13 1600
14 180
15 600
16 240
17 380
18 2300
19 1100
20 520

21 1200
22 560
23 2700
24 3000
25 5000
26 1300
27 4000
28 1500
29 3500
30 2600

Challenge

| 95 | 96 | 97 | 98 | 99 | 100 |

You will need a number line or a 100 cm ruler (a metre stick marked with centimetres), and a few small items to use as markers (cm cubes, counters, buttons – anything small).
If you use a number line on the wall, you will also need some Blu-tack.
Place a marker by the number 100. Halve the number and place another marker. Keep on halving until you reach an odd number. Look at the positions of the markers. What is happening? Can you explain why? Repeat, starting with other high even numbers. Does the same thing happen?

Unit 44
Problems 8

Last week Tim was kidnapped by aliens. When they brought him back to earth, they gave him a present called 'Special Growth Tonic'.
On Monday night, he gave some to his hamster. Harry the hamster was his usual 10 cm long on Monday morning.
By Tuesday night, he had doubled in length to 20 cm. Tim had to let him out of the cage and put him in the shed.
By Wednesday night, Harry had doubled again to 40 cm long, and the dog was looking worried!

1 **(a)** How long was Harry the hamster on Thursday?
   (b) How long was he on Friday, the same day the dog left home?
   (c) How long was he on Saturday, when he had to be moved into the garage?

2 Tim mixed some tonic in his dad's face wash on Monday.
Dad's beard was only 1 cm long. One day later, his beard had doubled in length.
   (a) How long was it by Wednesday night?
   (b) How long was it by Friday night?
   (c) How long was it on Sunday night?
   (d) Dad's chin is 2 metres above the ground. On what day will his beard reach the floor?

Tim is worried. He pours the rest of the tonic away, over the front lawn!
The grass is 7 cm long.
3 How long was the grass after:
   (a) one day
   (b) two days
   (c) three days
   (d) four days?

4 They didn't need downstairs curtains after five days. How long was the grass?
5 On the sixth day they didn't need any curtains. How long was the grass?

Tim woke up to the sound of a 5 m-long hamster eating the grass. By 1 o'clock it was just 960 cm long. Harry ate half the length of the grass each hour.
6 How long was the grass at:
   (a) 2 o'clock
   (b) 3 o'clock
   (c) 4 o'clock
   (d) 5 o'clock
   (e) 6 o'clock
   (f) 7 o'clock
   (g) 8 o'clock?

Unit 45
Multiplying by 10 and 100

To multiply a number by 10, move the digits one column to the left.
With a whole number, put a zero in the units column to 'push' the digits over.
Example $10 \times 34 \rightarrow 340$
To multiply a number by 100, we use two zeros to
push the digits two columns to the left.
Example $100 \times 34 = 3400$
Complete the following equations, using one or two zeros to push the digits to the left.

1 $45 \times 10 =$
2 $25 \times 100 =$
3 $392 \times 10 =$
4 $36 \times 100 =$
5 $435 \times 100 =$
6 $648 \times 100 =$
7 $122 \times 10 =$
8 $450 \times 10 =$
9 $12 \times 10 =$
10 $86 \times 100 =$

11 $367 \times 100 =$
12 $45 \times 100 =$
13 $78 \times 10 =$
14 $64 \times 100 =$
15 $780 \times 10 =$
16 $999 \times 100 =$
17 $32 \times 10 =$
18 $78 \times 100 =$
19 $365 \times 10 =$
20 $382 \times 100 =$

21 $463 \times 100 =$
22 $207 \times 100 =$
23 $73 \times 100 =$
24 $94 \times 10 =$
25 $52 \times 10 =$
26 $65 \times 10 =$
27 $88 \times 100 =$
28 $986 \times 10 =$
29 $500 \times 100 =$
30 $479 \times 10 =$

Challenge

You need a page of squared paper and a strip of paper with
the same-sized squares. Cut out the shape shown in the
picture and snip between the two squares at the bottom.
Label it with **HTU** and **00** as shown.
Fold up the two squares and label them on the back **T** and **U**.
Now write a two-digit number on your page.
Hold on to the top of the slip of paper and place it above
the numbers so that the **T** and **U** are over the tens and units.
To multiply by 10, slide the HTU multiplier one square to the
right, and fold down the **U** to show a **0**.
To multiply by 100, fold down the **T** and the **U** to show **00**
and slide your multiplier two squares to the right.

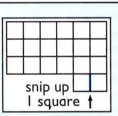

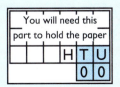

Unit 46

Doubling and Halving Short Cuts

Here is a good short cut for multiplying a pair of numbers when one is a larger, even number. Before multiplying, you double one number and halve the other.

Example 3 × 18 =   Double the 3 and halve the 18 → 6 × 9 = 54
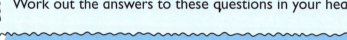
4 × 14 =   Double the 4 and halve the 14 → 8 × 7 = 56
16 × 5 =   Halve the 16 and double the 5 → 8 × 10 = 80

Work out the answers to these questions in your head.

1 4 × 16 =
2 5 × 18 =
3 5 × 20 =
4 14 × 2 =
5 18 × 2 =
6 5 × 16 =

7 4 × 16 =
8 3 × 14 =
9 3 × 16 =
10 5 × 14 =
11 20 × 4 =
12 18 × 3 =

13 3 × 20 =
14 4 × 18 =
15 4 × 14 =
16 3 × 18 =
17 4 × 20 =
18 2 × 16 =

With larger numbers, you may have to 'count on' from the end of your times tables.

Example
4 × 26 = 8 × 13   8 × 10 = 80   Count on 3 more 8s   80 + 8 + 8 + 8 = 104

19 3 × 22 =
20 6 × 30 =
21 3 × 24 =
22 7 × 30 =

23 5 × 22 =
24 5 × 26 =
25 5 × 30 =
26 3 × 26 =

27 4 × 30 =
28 6 × 26 =
29 4 × 28 =
30 6 × 22 =

Challenge

Can you alter this short cut so that it will work with a larger number that is odd?

Example   4 × 17 =

Try out your ideas to see if they work.
You might need a calculator to check your answers.

46

Unit 47
More Multiplication Short Cuts

Here are some more tips to make multiplication problems easier.
- You can reverse the order of the numbers: 14 × 4 is the same as 4 × 14.
- Moving the digits in a number one column to the left will multiply it by 10.
- 20 is 2 × 10, so to multiply by 20, multiply by 2 **and** move one column to the left.
- To multiply by 100, move the digits two columns to the left.
- You can split up a number: 17 is 8 + 9, so 6 × 17 is the same as 6 × 8 plus 6 × 9.
- You can multiply the tens and units separately:
  56 × 4 is the same as 50 × 4 plus 6 × 4.
  Use your knowledge of number facts and short cuts to complete the following questions **in your head**.

1 20 × 7 =
2 19 × 10 =
3 15 × 5 =
4 18 × 4 =
5 3 × 50 =
6 5 × 12 =
7 35 × 100 =
8 30 × 8 =
9 50 × 8 =
10 500 × 8 =

11 21 × 4 =
12 34 × 6 =
13 4 × 24 =
14 16 × 6 =
15 200 × 6 =
16 14 × 4 =
17 33 × 3 =
18 40 × 4 =
19 50 × 7 =
20 9 × 25 =

21 7 × 17 =
22 25 × 7 =
23 20 × 7 =
24 14 × 30 =
25 24 × 9 =
26 19 × 5 =
27 101 × 9 =
28 75 × 11 =
29 50 × 50 =
30 7 × 40 =

Challenge

Choose one of the most difficult problems from above that you managed to work out in your head.
Copy it down and use a colouring pencil or a coloured felt tip to write down how you did it.

Example

101 × 9
100 + 1
100 × 9 = 900 + 1 × 9 = 909

There may be more than one short cut for solving the problem. If there is, write that down too. Any short cut that works for you is fine.

Unit 48

Using Multiplication Short Cuts

Solve these problems in your head, using your knowledge of multiplication tables and short-cut methods.

1. 15 × 6 =
2. 17 × 10 =
3. 50 × 6 =
4. 18 × 7 =
5. 5 × 50 =
6. 6 × 12 =
7. 29 × 100 =
8. 30 × 9 =
9. 40 × 7 =
10. 30 × 7 =

11. 31 × 3 =
12. 32 × 6 =
13. 4 × 23 =
14. 20 × 12 =
15. 300 × 6 =
16. 16 × 4 =
17. 33 × 4 =
18. 500 × 6 =
19. 14 × 6 =
20. 11 × 25 =

21. 9 × 17 =
22. 25 × 11 =
23. 19 × 9 =
24. 75 × 11 =
25. 50 × 9 =
26. 17 × 5 =
27. 99 × 9 =
28. 11 × 30 =
29. 50 × 20 =
30. 9 × 40 =

Challenge

Choose one of the most difficult problems from above that you managed to work out in your head.
Copy it down and use a colouring pencil to write down how you did it and other ways you could have done it.

Example   11 × 30   11 = 10 + 1, so 10 × 30 = 300 plus 1 × 30 = 330
or 11 × 3 = 33 and move one column to the left = 330

Any short cut that works for you is fine.
Choose some other difficult problems and make notes of how you solved them.

Unit 49
Problems 9

Use multiplication short cuts to solve these problems mentally (do them in your head).

1. Yahimba is going to rewire the house. Work out the cost of:
   (a) 250 cable clips @ 2p each (the symbol @ means 'at')
   (b) 75 metres of cable @ 17p per metre
   (c) 100 metres of cable @ 34p per metre
   (d) 20 plug sockets @ £5.99 each
   (e) 11 light switches @ £1.95 each
   (f) 9 light bulb sockets @ £2.05 each
   (g) 9 'ceiling roses' @ £0.95 each
   (h) 50 floorboard nails @ 3p each.

2. A plumber repairs the nailed-through water pipe. Work out the cost of:
   (a) travelling expenses, 20 miles @ 44p per mile
   (b) 2 pipe joints @ £1.99
   (c) 3 metres of copper pipe @ £4.25 a metre
   (d) 5 hours of labour @ £25 per hour.

3. How many hours did it take Yahimba to finish the job, working $9\frac{1}{2}$ hours a day for five days?

4. How much would it have cost for a qualified electrician, working for four days @ £95 a day?

5. Yahimba and Pravin decide to decorate the house themselves.
   Find the cost of:
   (a) 10 rolls of wallpaper @ £7.95 a roll
   (b) 8 rolls of wallpaper @ £6.25 a roll
   (c) 5 rolls of wallpaper @ £10.10 a roll
   (d) 30 litres of emulsion paint @ £4.99 per 5 litre tin.

6. How much would it cost to replace the following?
   (a) $6\frac{1}{2}$ metres of stair carpet @ £11 per metre
   (b) 12 square metres of bedroom carpet @ £6.20 per m^2
   (c) 10 square metres of bedroom carpet @ £4.95 per m^2
   (d) 7 square metres of bedroom carpet @ £5.50 per m^2
   (e) 15 square metres of lounge carpet @ £16.00 per m^2
   (f) 4 square metres of bathroom carpet @ £7.50 per m^2.

Unit 50
Tally Charts and Frequency Tables

Tallying is a useful way of counting. It is just like counting on your fingers, but you write it down.

The first four fingers are written as sticks like this. ||||

The fifth finger (your thumb) goes across to make five. ||||̸

It is easy to count in fives, then add on 'loose' tally marks. ||||̸ ||||̸ |||

Write in the totals of these sets of tally marks.

1. ||||̸ ||||̸
2. ||||̸ |
3. ||||̸ ||
4. ||||̸ ||||̸ |
5. ||||̸ ||||̸
6. ||||̸ |||
7. ||||̸ ||||
8. ||||̸ ||||̸
9. ||||̸ ||||̸ ||
10. ||||̸ ||||̸ |
11. ||||̸ ||||̸
12. ||||̸ ||||̸ ||||

Draw tally marks for the totals given below.

13. = 7
14. = 9
15. = 6
16. = 15
17. = 14
18. = 12
19. = 16
20. = 13
21. = 17
22. = 25
23. = 19
24. = 22

When we count up using tally marks, we can put the totals into a **frequency table**. Use the tally marks from this traffic survey to complete the frequency table below.

Traffic passing our school in 30 minutes
- bicycles ||||̸
- motorbikes ||
- cars ||||̸ ||||̸ ||||̸
- buses |
- small vans ||||̸ ||||̸ |
- big vans ||||̸ ||
- lorries

Vehicle type	Total
bicycles	
motorbikes	
cars	
buses	
small vans	
big vans	
lorries	

Challenge

Asking only the people who sit at your table, conduct a simple survey.

Example What sport do you most like to watch?
What is your favourite flavour of drink?

Collect the data by tallying. Put the totals into a frequency table.

Unit 51
Bar Charts

When we have collected data and put them into a frequency table, we can use the table to make a **bar chart**. This makes it easier to compare things.

1 Copy this frequency table and bar chart.

Drink	Number
chocomilk	5
coffee	3
milk	4
pop	8
squash	6
tea	2

(a) How many children prefer hot drinks?
(b) How many children prefer cold drinks?
(c) List the drinks in order, starting with the most popular (descending order).

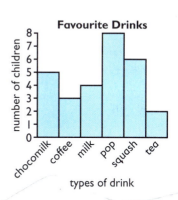

2 Look at this bar chart and answer the questions.

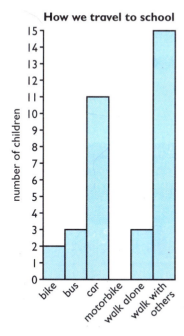

(a) What does it show?
(b) List the types of travel in descending order.
(c) How many cycle to school?
(d) How many walk to school?
(e) How many travel to school in a vehicle?
(f) How many travel with someone else?
(g) How many children were asked?
(h) Why **might** cycling be unpopular?
(i) Suggest which children might have a safer journey.

3 Use this frequency table to make a bar chart. Remember to give it a title and labels.

Pet Ownership

Pet	Number
bird	4
cat	10
dog	6
fish	7
hamster	4
no pet	3

Challenge

Conduct a survey of your own (ask your teacher first). Collect your data.

Make a frequency chart. Draw a bar chart of the results.

Unit 52
Venn Diagrams

This is a way of showing information called a **Venn diagram**. It places sets of names or items inside rings. Some names or items may be in more than one set, or in no set at all.

1 Use this Venn diagram to answer the questions.

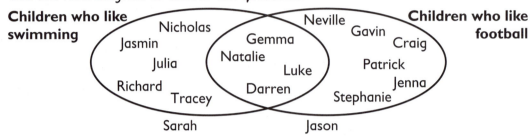

(a) Which children don't like either football or swimming?
(b) How many children like swimming but not football?
(c) How many children like football but not swimming?
(d) Which children like both?
(e) How many children are there in this survey?

2 Use the information below to make a Venn diagram showing:
children who like to read fiction books (stories)
children who like to read non-fiction books (other books)

Aarif reads any books about pirates
Natalie likes Roald Dahl stories
Darren likes football stories
Rob doesn't like books
Matanga likes books about history
Nicholas likes science and science fiction books
Patrick likes Harry Potter stories
John likes stories about cowboys

Sarah likes stories and books about athletics
Kate likes horror stories
Stephanie doesn't like books
Medha reads stories and non-fiction about football
Luke's hobby is fishing and he reads about it

3 Make up five questions that you could ask about the information in your Venn diagram.

Challenge

Conduct a survey of your own, asking people just two things, then make a Venn diagram to show the results.

Unit 53
Carroll Diagrams

This is called a **Carroll diagram**. It is another way of giving information that has been sorted. The children were asked about the sorts of books they like. Their names were put into a row to show if they prefer books about sport or not, and into a column to show if they prefer fiction (stories) or non-fiction books.

	Fiction	Non-fiction
About sport	Sudi, Sarah	Julia, Tracey, Sameer
Not about sport	Sam, Jyoti, Patrick, Ninesh, Natalie, Richard	Gavin, Jasmin, Gemma, Pradeep

1 Answer these questions by looking at the Carroll diagram.
   (a) How many children prefer fiction books?
   (b) How many children prefer books **not** about sport?
   (c) Which children prefer non-fiction books about sport?
   (d) What does Pradeep prefer?
   (e) What does Tracey prefer?

2 The school is sorting the children out to see who might be able to take part in the swimming gala. The swimmers have a letter **S** by their name. Copy this Carroll diagram and put the children's names in the correct section.

	Can swim	Can't swim
Boys		
Girls		

Boys
Tim S   Yusuf S   Nicholas   Rushanara   Julia
Vijay   Luke S   Patrick S   Jasmin S   Nat S
Michael   Neil   Ilesh   Jen S   Abi

Girls
Stephanie S
Geraldine

Challenge

Make a Carroll diagram of your own. You may not need to ask anyone for information if you choose something you know about.

Example

	Hot	Cold
Food		
Drink		

Unit 54
Problems 10

On this page there is a bar chart, a Venn diagram and a Carroll diagram. Study them carefully and answer the questions.

1. How many children like to watch:
   (a) children's programmes
   (b) comedy
   (c) films
   (d) news
   (e) soaps
   (f) sport?

2. Which type of programme is:
   (a) most popular
   (b) least popular?

3. How many children took part in the survey?
4. How many creatures eat meat?
5. How many eat plants?
6. How many eat both plants and meat?
7. Which four-legged creatures eat only meat?
8. Which is the smallest plant-eater?
9. Copy the Venn diagram and add some more creatures. You may have to check where to put them.

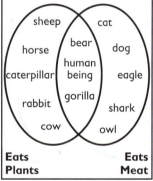

	In Europe	Not in Europe
Country	France Italy Belgium Spain Britain Germany	Canada Brazil Thailand India Korea China
Towns and cities	Oslo Walsall Lyon Rome Berne Bruges	Cairo Tokyo New York Lima Tripoli Karachi

10. Name:
    (a) two towns in Europe
    (b) two towns not in Europe
    (c) three non-European countries
    (d) three European countries
    (e) three countries that begin with **B**.

11. Look at the towns and cities in the Carroll diagram. Use an atlas to find out which countries they are in.

12. Copy the Carroll diagram, leaving yourself room to add more countries and towns.

Unit 55
Length, Mass and Capacity

We measure **length** in **metres** (you can write just **m** for metres).
1 m = 100 centimetres.
For shorter lengths, we use **centimetres** (you can write just **cm** for centimetres).
100 cm = 1 metre.
A metre is **about** the length of two of your strides, and a centimetre is **about** the width of the tip of your little finger. Complete the conversions below.
Example $1\frac{1}{2}$ metres = 150 cm   5 m = 500 cm   8 m = 800 cm

1 2 m = ⬤ cm
2 ⬤ m = 400 cm
3 $2\frac{1}{2}$ m = ⬤ cm
4 ⬤ m = 600 cm
5 4 m = ⬤ cm
6 $3\frac{1}{2}$ m = ⬤ cm
7 ⬤ m = 300 cm
8 $5\frac{1}{2}$ m = ⬤ cm
9 ⬤ m = 350 cm

Draw straight lines in your book of these lengths: **10** 5 cm   **11** 10 cm   **12** 15 cm

We measure **mass** (weight) in **grams** (shortened to **g**) and **kilograms** (shortened to **kg**). **1000 grams = 1 kilogram**. 'Kilo' means 1000.
Complete the conversions below.
Example $1\frac{1}{2}$ kg = 1500 g   5 kg = 5000 g   8 kg = 8000 g

13 $2\frac{1}{2}$ kg = ⬤ g
14 1000 g = ⬤ kg
15 3500 g = ⬤ kg
16 ⬤ g = 4 kg
17 $\frac{1}{2}$ kg = ⬤ g
18 $\frac{1}{4}$ kg = ⬤ g
19 200 g + 300 g = ⬤ kg
20 2 kg + 500 g = ⬤ kg
21 $\frac{3}{4}$ kg = ⬤ g

Capacity is a measure of the space inside a container. A cube-shaped container measuring 10 cm tall, 10 cm wide and 10 cm deep has a capacity of **1 litre (1 l)**. For smaller amounts, we use **millilitres (ml)**. **1 litre = 1000 ml**.
Complete the conversions below.
Example $1\frac{1}{2}$ l = 1500 ml   5 l = 5000 ml   8 l = 8000 ml

22 $\frac{1}{2}$ l = ⬤ ml
23 ⬤ l = 2000 ml
24 $2\frac{1}{2}$ l = ⬤ ml
25 3000 ml = ⬤ l
26 4 l = ⬤ ml
27 ⬤ l = 5000 ml
28 500 ml + $\frac{1}{2}$ l = ⬤ l
29 $\frac{1}{4}$ l = ⬤ ml
30 $\frac{3}{4}$ l = ⬤ ml

Challenge

If 1 litre of pure water weighs 1 kilogram, how many millilitres of water weigh 1 gram? If your teacher will let you, weigh a litre of water and see if it weighs 1 kg. You will have to weigh the container on its own and subtract this from the total weight. Make a 1 ml measure. One way is to push a 1 cm cube into plasticine then carefully remove it.

Unit 56
Measuring with Decimals

To change metres to cm, you need to multiply by 100.
To do this, you move the digits two columns to the left.
You may have to put in zeros to fill the empty columns.
To change centimetres into metres, you divide by 100,
moving the digits two columns to the right.
Make sure there is a decimal point to the right of the
units before you start.
Make the conversions below by multiplying or dividing by 100.

1 1·5 m = ◯ cm   **4** 325 cm = ◯ m   **7** 2·75 m = ◯ cm

2 200 cm = ◯ m   **5** 3·25 m = ◯ cm   **8** 185 cm = ◯ m

3 2·50 m = ◯ cm   **6** 250 cm = ◯ m   **9** 7·21 m = ◯ cm

To change **kilograms** to **grams**, or **litres** to **millilitres**, you multiply by 1000.
You do this by moving the digits three columns to the left. To change **g** to **kg**, or
ml to **l**, you divide by 1000, moving the digits three columns to the right.
Make the conversions below by multiplying or dividing by 1000.

10 2 kg = ◯ g   **17** 1725 ml = ◯ l   **24** 1245 ml = ◯ l

11 1 l = ◯ ml   **18** 4·75 kg = ◯ g   **25** 11·722 kg = ◯ g

12 1500 g = ◯ kg   **19** 0·75 l = ◯ ml   **26** 1534 g = ◯ kg

13 2500 ml = ◯ l   **20** 1·75 l = ◯ ml   **27** 2955 g = ◯ kg

14 2·5 kg = ◯ g   **21** 0·2 kg = ◯ g   **28** 3525 g = ◯ kg

15 1·25 l = ◯ ml   **22** 330 ml = ◯ l   **29** 40·861 l = ◯ ml

16 2750 g = ◯ kg   **23** 3·252 kg = ◯ g   **30** 538 ml = ◯ l

Challenge

Turn back to the challenge on page 45, which showed you how to make a paper
device for multiplying by 10 to 100.
Can you adapt the idea to make a device that will multiply by 100 or 1000?
It would be useful for doing conversions like some of the ones above.
Can you use it to divide by 100 or 1000? Perhaps you need to change the design.

Unit 57
Scales

> To measure something accurately, we use a scale, either along a straight line or curved around a dial. Sometimes what we are measuring comes between the numbers and we have to look at smaller divisions.
>
> **Example**   This rod measures $7\frac{1}{2}$ cm.
>
> Different scales have different-sized divisions.
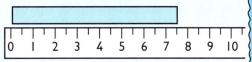

1 Write down the marked readings on this scale.

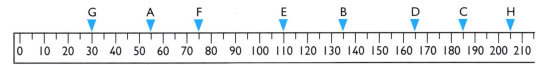

2 What is the value of the smallest divisions on this scale?

3 Write down what is shown by A, B, C, D, E, F, G and H on this scale.

4 How many grams are represented by the smallest division on this scale?

5 Write down the readings A to J on this dial.

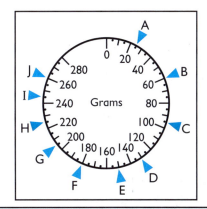

6 How many grams are shown by the smallest divisions on the dial?

Challenge

Look for some things that have a scale or dial on them.
Write down what each scale measures (length, weight and so on) and the units it measures in (cm, kg, °C, and so on).
On each scale, what is the value of the smallest division?
What is the range (what the scale starts and ends with)?

Unit 58
Problems 11

1. Phil Ittup's car has a fuel tank with a capacity of 55 litres.
   He always fills the tank up when he buys fuel.
   How much is left in the tank if he has to put in:
   (a) 33 litres
   (b) 45·500 litres
   (c) 42·440 litres
   (d) 37·250 litres?

2. Change each of the litre amounts left in the tank in question 1 into millilitres.

3. Change each of the litre amounts put into the tank in question 1 into millilitres.

4. Sweeny's sausage machine makes one giant 10 metre-long sausage, which has to be split up into normal-sized sausages.
   (a) How many centimetres long is the giant sausage?
   (b) How many 16 cm sausages could Sweeny get from it?
   (c) How many 20 cm sausages could he get from it?
   (d) How many 8 cm sausages could he get from it?

5. SafeCo supermarket sells pop in these sizes:

   $\frac{1}{3}$ litre cans for 25p

   $\frac{1}{2}$ litre bottles for 35p

   2 litre bottles for 95p

   (a) Which is the cheapest price per litre?
   (b) How many litres of pop could you buy for £4·00 if you bought only cans?
   (c) How many litres of pop could you buy for £4·00 if you bought only $\frac{1}{2}$ litre bottles?
   (d) How many litres of pop could you buy for £4·00 if you bought only 2 litre bottles?

6. SafeCo supermarket sells bags of sweets in these sizes:
   250 g for 85p   500 g for £1·65   1 kg for £3·40
   (a) How much would it cost to buy 3 kg of sweets in 250 g bags?
   (b) How much would it cost to buy 3 kg of sweets in 500 g bags?
   (c) Which size of bag gives the best value?
   (d) How many grams of sweets could you buy with £4·50, buying only 250 g bags?
   (e) How many grams of sweets could you buy with £4·50, buying only 500 g bags?
   (f) How many grams of sweets could you buy with £4·50, buying only 1 kg bags?

Unit 59
Units of Time

We use different units of time, depending on how much time we are measuring.
1 year = all of these: **365 days, 12 months, 52 weeks**
A year is the time it takes the earth to orbit once around the sun, causing us to have spring, summer, autumn and winter.
1 week = both of these: **7 days, 168 hours**   **1 hour** = **60 minutes**
1 minute = **60 seconds**   Use this information to complete the time conversions below.

1. 2 hours = ⬡ minutes
2. 2 minutes = ⬡ seconds
3. 2 years = ⬡ months
4. 2 days = ⬡ hours
5. 2 years = ⬡ days
6. 2 years = ⬡ weeks
7. 4 minutes = ⬡ seconds
8. 2 weeks = ⬡ days
9. 5 minutes = ⬡ seconds
10. 4 years = ⬡ months
11. 5 hours = ⬡ minutes
12. 4 weeks = ⬡ days
13. 3 years = ⬡ weeks
14. $\frac{3}{4}$ of an hour = ⬡ minutes
15. $1\frac{1}{2}$ years = ⬡ months
16. 4 years = ⬡ days
17. 10 weeks = ⬡ days
18. $1\frac{1}{2}$ hours = ⬡ minutes
19. 3 weeks = ⬡ days
20. 5 days = ⬡ hours
21. $2\frac{1}{2}$ hours = ⬡ minutes
22. $2\frac{1}{2}$ minutes = ⬡ seconds
23. $1\frac{3}{4}$ hours = ⬡ minutes
24. $1\frac{3}{4}$ minutes = ⬡ seconds
25. $1\frac{1}{2}$ minutes = ⬡ seconds
26. 6 years = ⬡ months
27. 6 years = ⬡ days
28. $1\frac{3}{4}$ years = ⬡ months
29. $\frac{1}{2}$ a year = ⬡ weeks
30. 8 days = ⬡ hours

Challenge

Try to find answers to the following questions.
You will find library non-fiction books useful.
If you have a computer CD-ROM encyclopaedia, try that first.
(a) Does the earth take exactly 365 days to orbit around the sun?
(b) What is a leap year and why do we have them?
(c) What is a lunar month?
(d) How is it different from a calendar month?
(e) How many lunar months do we have in a year?

Unit 60
Reading the Time

We measure the passage of time during the day using clocks and watches. There are two types of display, digital and analogue. A **digital** display uses changing numerals. An **analogue** display (a dial) uses two hands (or fingers).

| The whole hours that have gone | | The whole minutes that have gone since the last whole hour | The hour hand moves around the dial once every 12 hours, twice a day. | | The longer minute hand moves around once every hour. It takes 5 minutes to pass each numeral. |

When you read the time in hours and minutes using an analogue display, you can use a few short cuts.
Halving the clock – half the dial is 30 minutes
Quartering the clock, 3 numerals = 15 minutes
Try counting around in 5s, then add on any more minutes.

1 Copy down these digital clock displays and write the time in words next to them. Remember, there is often more than one way to say the time.

Example It is 8:50. It is fifty minutes past 8. It is ten minutes to nine.

(a), (b), (c), (d), (e), (f)

(g), (h), (i), (j), (k), (l)

2 Draw a clock face to show each of the times in question 1(a) to (f).

3 Read these times and write them down like you did for question 1. They are all before 12:00 midday.

(a) (b) (c)

(d) (e) (f)

Challenge

Write down important times in a normal day for you. Work out how long you spend eating, sleeping, working, playing, watching television and so on.

Unit 61
Calendars

We use calendars to record time in days. We use them to plan ahead, such as when we are going to do something special. On a calendar you can count in months, weeks and days.

1 Write down the names of each month, in the correct order. Make sure you spell them correctly.

2 Write down the number of days in each month.

3 Look at the calendar months for this year.
   (a) How many Sundays are there in January?
   (b) How many Sundays are there in May?
   (c) How many Saturdays are there in January?
   (d) How many Saturdays are there in May?

Often we write the date like this.   the 16th   May (the 5th month)   1999
16.05.99

4 Write out these dates in full and say which day they fall on. Use this year's calendar
   (a) 30.01
   (b) 02.08
   (c) 15.05
   (d) 14.11
   (e) 30.11
   (f) 14.02
   (g) 23.04
   (h) 28.03

5 Use the calendar to count on how many weeks there are from:
   (a) 1st March to 12th April
   (b) 19th June to 30th October
   (c) 14th July to 20th October
   (d) 16th November to 28th December
   (e) 23rd December to 6th January
   (f) 6th November to 15th January.

Challenge

Pick two dates at random from the calendar pages. How many days are there between them?
Copy one of the months, but change it so that the days of the week go down instead of across.

Unit 62
Problems 12

1. (a) What was the date ten days ago?
   (b) What day did it fall on?

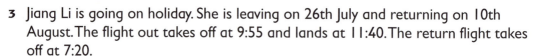

2. (a) What day will it be in ten days' time?
   (b) What day will it fall on?

3. Jiang Li is going on holiday. She is leaving on 26th July and returning on 10th August. The flight out takes off at 9:55 and lands at 11:40. The return flight takes off at 7:20.
   (a) How many days is she going to be away for?
   (b) She has to book in at the airport 50 minutes before each flight. What times will these be?
   (c) How long does the flight out last?
   (d) The return flight will take the same length of time. When will it land?

4. Before going away, she set the video to record her favourite programmes. She set the start time 5 minutes before the programme was due to start, and the end time 5 minutes after the programme was due to end. What start and stop times did she use for:
   (a) a 30 minute programme due to start at 7:30
   (b) a 45 minute programme due to start at 6:25
   (c) a 75 minute programme due to start at 8:15?

5. Ilesh enters a pie-eating contest.
   (a) If it takes him $1\frac{1}{2}$ minutes to eat his first pie, how long might it take him to eat ten?
   (b) He finds each pie takes 5 seconds longer than the one before it. How long does it take to eat five pies?

6. After recovering, Ilesh goes to the gym. He spends 10 minutes warming up, 70 minutes exercising, 5 minutes cooling down and 20 minutes showering and getting changed.
   (a) How long does he spend at the gym?
   (b) If he arrives at 7:30, at what time does he leave?

7. Ratbag the cat only seems to do three things all day. How long does he spend:
   (a) eating   7:30 till 7:40, 12:00 till 12:07, 5:45 till 5:55, and 10:05 till 10:11
   (b) outside   7:40 till 8:30, 12:10 till 12:50, 5:05 till 5:54 and 10:12 till 11:00
   (c) sleeping   all the other times (remember this is out of 24 hours)?

Unit 63
2-D Shapes

This page is about 2-D shapes.
If a shape has three straight sides and three angles, it must be a **triangle**.

If a shape has four straight sides, it is called a **quadrilateral**.

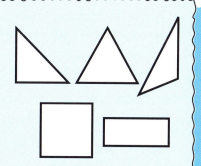

Other straight-sided shapes include:
pentagon – five sides; **hexagon** – six sides; **octagon** – eight sides.

1. Write down the name of each shape below and describe its sides and angles – how many are there, are they equal, and so on.

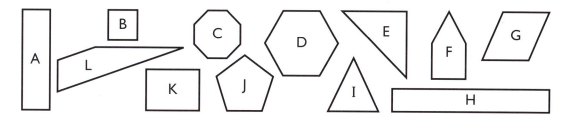

2. Using squared paper, draw and label these shapes:
   (a) a quadrilateral with no right angles
   (b) a pentagon with three right angles
   (c) a triangle with a right angle and two sides the same length
   (d) a semi-circle
   (e) a triangle with all three sides different lengths
   (f) a circle.

3. How many sides does:
   (a) the semi-circle have
   (b) the circle have?

Challenge

Draw a rectangle and divide it up into smaller, straight-edged shapes. Cut them out carefully. Now can you sort them into sets of triangles, quadrilaterals, and so on? Make up other ways to sort your shapes.

Unit 64
3-D Shapes

This page is about 3-D shapes.
They have **three dimensions** – height, width and length.
If a solid is the same shape and size all the way through, we call it a **prism**.
If it is the same shape all the way through but narrows to a point, it is a **pyramid**.

1 Name the solid shapes that have been drawn below, and describe each shape to explain how you know it is what you say it is, for example it is a cube because all six faces are square.

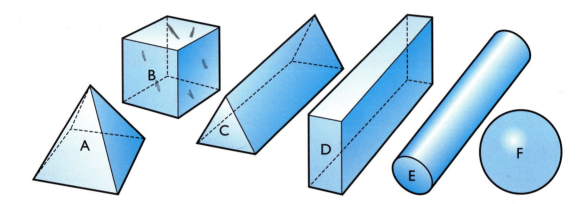

2 Which of the shapes:
   (a) has six faces all the same size and shape
   (b) has three rectangular faces and two triangular faces
   (c) has two flat circular faces and one curved face
   (d) has four triangular faces and one square face
   (e) has two square faces and four oblong faces
   (f) has only one face
   (g) will roll?

Challenge

Using squared paper, draw out the 'net' of one of these 'solid' shapes.
If you get it right, you should be able to cut it out and fold it up into the solid shape.

Unit 65
Symmetry and Reflections

Use squared paper or a squared paper exercise book to do this page.

1. Draw these objects and put in one line of symmetry like this: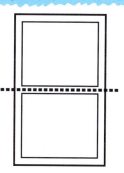
   (a) one of your classroom windows
   (b) a cupboard or a classroom door
   (c) this shape.

   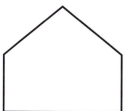

2. Draw these shapes and put in two lines of symmetry like this:
   (a) a rectangle eight squares tall and four squares wide
   (b) a rectangle four squares tall and five squares wide
   (c) a square with a circle inside it like this one:
   (d) a hexagon
   (e) a shape of your own.

3. Here are some half pictures. Draw in the line of symmetry, copy the half that is shown here, then add the missing half.

   (a) 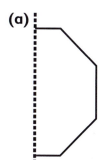   (b) 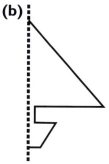   (c)

Challenge

Draw a house front that is symmetrical, and where every feature is also symmetrical.

Unit 66
Position and Movement

1. Draw a rectangle in your book.
   (a) Label the horizontal and vertical lines.
   (b) Draw in and label both diagonal lines.

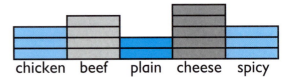

2. Copy this set of stairs.
   (a) Number the stairs in **ascending** order (going up).
   (b) Draw it again with the stairs numbered in **descending** order (going down).

3. A shop stacks its boxes of crisps like this.
   Each flavour is in a different column.

   chicken   beef   plain   cheese   spicy

   (a) How many columns are there?
   (b) How many complete rows are there?
   (c) Which column has most boxes?
   (d) Which is the shortest column?

4. Draw a rectangle 12 cm wide and 6 cm tall.
   Mark a + in the centre of it.
   Draw a simple compass rose in the top right-hand corner.

   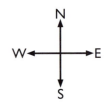

   Use the compass points to draw out this route, starting from the centre mark +.

   (a) Go north for 2 cm.
   (b) Go east 5 cm.
   (c) Go south 4 cm.
   (d) Go west 10 cm.
   (e) Go north 3 cm.
   (f) Go east 3 cm.
   (g) Go south 1 cm.
   (h) Go east 2 cm.

5. The children are playing a game, standing in a circle.
   (a) Copy this plan of where they are standing.
   (b) Draw a box behind Kim.
   (c) Draw a hoop in front of Steph.
   (d) Who is the fifth person from Kim going clockwise?
   (e) Who is the fourth person from Lisa going anticlockwise?
   (f) Who is standing opposite Becky?
   (g) Which two people is Lisa standing between?

   Kim
   Joanne   Dan
   Chris   Sara
   Steph   Lisa
       Luke   James
            Becky

Challenge

Draw a simple plan of your route to school.
Draw a plan of your table, marking on where everything is at the moment

Unit 67
Coordinate Grids

1 Write down the coordinates of the shapes on the grid. Remember to use the **column** letter first, then the **row** number.

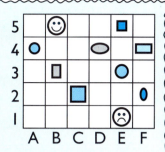

(a) The happy face is in
(b) The sad face is in
(c) The large circle is in
(d) The small circle is in
(e) The small square is in
(f) The small oval is in
(g) The large square is in
(h) The small rectangle is in
(i) The large rectangle is in
(j) The large oval is in

2 Draw an empty coordinate grid similar to the one above. You will need six columns labelled **A** to **F** and five rows labelled **1** to **5**. Now draw these in the correct places:

(a) a scary face in A4
(b) a mouse in B3
(c) a fish in C1
(d) a ball in D4
(e) yourself in E2
(f) your teacher in F5
(g) a house in A1
(h) a cloud in C4
(i) a doll in D3
(j) a book in E5
(k) a bird in B5
(l) a triangle in F2.

Challenge

Making a secret code grid

Here is a coded message using this code grid:

E2, C6, A4, C5   A4, C5   E4, E6, E6, A2   F4

	A	B	C	D	E	F
6	P	V	H	I	O	G
5	A	8	S	E	9	U
4	I	L	5	Z	B	3
3	W	7	D	R	O	N
2	K	Y	Q	2	T	F
1	4	M	6	C	X	1

To decode the message, find the correct letters or numerals from the coordinate grid.

Make your own code grid like this one. It doesn't have to be six columns of six rows, but you do need 36 squares altogether.

Put the letters and numerals in randomly. It might be helpful to use one colour for letters and another colour for numerals.

Encode your message using coordinates instead of letters. It is very hard to decode the message without a copy of the correct code grid.

Unit 68
Right Angles and Half Right Angles

If you look around the room, you will see many right angles. Try looking at the corners of windows, doors, walls, ceilings and books. For many things that we make, a right angle **is** the **'right angle'** for the corners. When we want to highlight a right angle, we put a small square in the corner like this.

1. Make a list of ten things in the room that have right angles.

2. (a) Draw a simple compass rose like this on a piece of paper. If you know which direction really is north, turn the compass around to face north.

   (b) Use a pencil as a pointer and place it on your compass rose facing north.
   Turn the pencil round clockwise through one right angle. Which direction is it facing?
   (c) Turn it through another right angle. Where is it facing now?
   (d) How many right-angle turns will you need to turn the pencil around one complete turn?
   (e) How many half right-angle turns would you need for a complete turn?

3. (a) Draw a square and fold it in two diagonally.
   (b) Cut it in two down the diagonal fold. You should now have two triangles, each with one right angle and two half right angles.
   (c) Mark the half right angles.
   (d) Turn one of the triangles and put them both together to make a larger triangle. Keep one half still and turn the other through two right angles.

4. (a) Make another pair of triangles by cutting a square in half.
   (b) Mark the half right angles.
   (c) Tear the half right angles off all four triangles and put them together so that the tips are all touching. Do they fit together?
   (d) Now try to do the same thing with the four right angles. Do they fit together?

Challenge

Get a square of sugar paper and cut it in half diagonally.
Cut one half in half again by cutting the right angle in half.
Take one of these halves and halve it again through the right angle.
Keep repeating this until you have a set of right-angled triangles, all different sizes except for the smallest pair. Now put it back together again!

Unit 69
Problems 13

1. A car is travelling north when it turns off left at a right angle.
   (a) What compass direction is it now travelling in?
   (b) How many more left turns like this does it need to make before it is travelling north again?

2. The driver finds that he is going the wrong way. He wants to go south instead of north.
   (a) How many left and right turns must he make to go back if his first turn is right?
   (b) How many left and right turns must he make to go back if his first turn is left?

3. (a) How many right angles are there on a clock face?
   (b) How long does it take the hour hand to turn through one right angle?
   (c) How long does it take the minute hand to turn through one right angle?
   (d) How long does it take the hour hand to turn through three right angles?
   (e) How long does it take the minute hand to turn through three right angles?

4. During a whole day (24 hours):
   (a) how many right angles does the hour hand turn through?
   (b) how many right angles does the minute hand turn through?

5. Darren is making a lidless box out of square panels. Each square needs metal corner pieces to make it stronger.
   (a) How many metal corner pieces does he need?
   (b) If he makes a lid as well, how many corner pieces will he need?

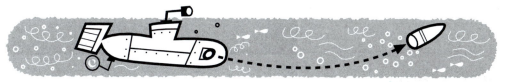

6. A submarine sends out a probe. The captain sees that the probe isn't going straight. It's turning left in a large circle.
   (a) What should the submarine captain do?
   (b) What will happen if he doesn't do anything?
   (c) Use a book or pencil case on your desk to represent the submarine. Pretend your pencil is the probe being fired and turning around to the left all the time. Were you right with your answer to (b)?